compile

* Style *

position

void TBitWindow

Crash Course in
Borland C++ 4

Namir C. Shammas

Crash Course in Borland C++ 4

© 1994 by Que© Corporation

Library of Congress Catalog No.: 94-65520

ISBN: 1-56529-773-3

97 96 95 94   8 7 6 5 4 3 2 1

Interpretation of the printing code: the rightmost double-digit number is the year of the book's printing; the rightmost single-digit number, the number of the book's printing. For example, a printing code of 94-1 shows that the first printing of the book occurred in 1994.

Publisher: David P. Ewing

Associate Publisher: Michael Miller

Publishing Director: Joseph B. Wikert

Managing Editor: Michael Cunningham

Product Marketing Manager: Ray Robinson

Dedication

To my special new friends Drew and Marlene Braytenbah

Credits

Acquisitions Editor
Angela Lee

Product Director
Bryan Gambrel

Production Editors
Lorna Gentry
Linda Seifert

Technical Editor
Robert Zigon

Figure Specialist
Wil Thebodeau

Book Designer
Amy Peppler-Adams

Cover Designer
Jean Bisesi

Editorial Assistant
Michelle Williams

Production Team
Gary Adair, Brad Chinn, Kim Cofer,
Meshell Dinn, Mark Enochs,
Teresa Forrester, Stephanie Gregory,
Jenny Kucera, Tim Montgomery,
Beth Rago, Marc Shecter,
Dennis Sheehan, Kris Simmons,
Greg Simsic, Carol Stamile,
Sue VandeWalle, Robert Wolf

Indexer
Jennifer Eberhardt

Composed in *ITC Garamond* and *MCPdigital* by Que Corporation

About the Author

Namir C. Shammas is a software engineer and an expert in object-oriented programming. He has authored and coauthored 30 books that deal with various programming languages. His other Que publications include *Using Borland C++* and *Using Visual C++*.

Acknowledgments

I would like to thank many people at Que for working with me on this book. Many thanks to Joe Wikert, who contacted me to write the book and was actively involved in editing it. I thank the technical editor, Robert Zigon, for his valuable comments and corrections. My gratitude to editor Lorna Gentry for ensuring the clarity of the text. Finally, many thanks to all the people at Que who were involved with the book.

Trademarks

All terms mentioned in this book that are known to be trademarks or service marks have been appropriately capitalized. Que cannot attest to the accuracy of this information. Use of a term in this book should not be regarded as affecting the validity of any trademark or service mark.

Contents at a Glance

Contents

10 Building Classes   123

11 Advanced Object-Oriented Programming   155

12 Stream File I/O   187

13 The C++ Exceptions   205

Introduction

This book teaches you to program with C++ in general and with Borland C++ 4 in particular. As part of the *Crash Course* book series, this book presents its topics at a fast pace, using relatively few and short examples.

This book takes a "no frills" approach to teaching the most important aspects of Borland C++ 4. You start learning the language in the first chapter. This book focuses on the key features of Borland C++ 4 so that the reader can begin writing practical applications in the shortest amount of time possible.

Who Should Use This Book?

This book is aimed at readers who want to learn the Borland C++ 4 programming language in the shortest amount of time possible. This group includes nonprogrammers who can learn in a fast-track environment as well as programmers who are switching to Borland C++ 4.

What You Should Know to Use This Book

This book assumes that you are familiar with common computer terminology. No time is wasted teaching you what an ASCII code is or how to write a batch file to start a C++ compiler. This book further assumes that readers have a good grasp of basic computing principles.

Organization of This Book

Crash Course in Borland C++ 4 is divided into 14 chapters.

Chapter 1 gives a brief background of C++ and a concise tour of the Borland C++ 4 integrated development environment (IDE).

Chapter 2 presents the first C++ program and explains the basic components of a C++ program. In addition, this chapter presents the compiler directives.

Chapter 3 talks about predefined data types, constants, variables, and operators.

Chapter 4 discusses the basic stream I/O and presents the functions that perform screen and cursor control.

Chapter 5 presents the decision-making constructs, which include the `if` and `switch` statements.

Chapter 6 talks about the various loops in C++. The loops include the versatile `for` loop as well as the conditional loops, `while` and `do-while`.

Chapter 7 discusses user-defined data types. These types include enumerated types, structures, and unions.

Chapter 8 presents reference variables, strings, and pointers. This chapter discusses pointers to simple types, strings, arrays, and structures.

Chapter 9 discusses C++ functions and covers a wide range of topics related to functions. Among these topics are function syntax, prototyping, function overloading, default arguments, and passing various kinds of parameters.

Chapter 10 looks at building a C++ class. This chapter discusses the various components of a class, including data members, member functions, friend functions, static members, and operators.

Chapter 11 presents more advanced topics related to class hierarchies. This chapter discusses class derivation, virtual functions, friend classes, and multiple inheritance.

Chapter 12 introduces the basics of file stream I/O using the C++ stream library. This chapter discusses sequential text I/O, sequential binary I/O, and random-access binary I/O.

Chapter 13 presents exceptions, the new error-handling mechanism that will become part of the C++ standard. The chapter presents the syntax and mechanism which supports exception handling.

Chapter 14 offers a sample Windows program created using the classes in the ObjectWindows Library (OWL). The sample program implements a command-oriented calculator.

Conventions Used

You benefit most from this book if you understand its design. The following list introduces you to the general conventions used throughout this book.

■ New terms and emphasized words are presented in *italics*.

■ Functions, commands, parameters, and the like are set in a special monospace text; for example, the `main()` function.

■ User responses that must be typed at program prompts appear in **monospace bold**; for example:

      Enter a string: **No strings attached!**

■ Placeholders (words that you replace with actual values) in code lines appear in *monospace italic*; for example:

      #define *constantName constantValue*

   In this example, you replace *constantName* and *constantValue* with the name and number appropriate to the program you are writing.

■ Full programs appear as listings with listing heads; code fragments appear alone within the text.

■ Shaded boxes, labeled "Syntax-at-a-Glance," appear throughout this book. This design feature provides easy language reference to the essential elements of Borland C++ 4 programming. By providing this helpful information, *Crash Course in Borland C++ 4* is not only a tutorial, but also a quick reference that will serve you for a long time to come. A sample Syntax-at-a-Glance box follows:

Syntax at a Glance

The *#include* Directive
The syntax of the #include directive is

        #include <*filename*>
        #include "*filename*"

The *filename* represents the name of the included file.

Example:
        #include <iostream.h>
        #include "string.hpp"

■ In addition to Syntax-at-a-Glance boxes, this book contains two other types of visual pointers.

Caution

Caution boxes warn you of problem areas, including situations in which you may introduce bugs into your program or crash your system.

 The pointing-hand icon directs your attention to paragraphs containing extra information. Many times, this information helps speed your learning process and provides you with shortcuts. Other times, it simply points to information important enough to deserve extra notice.

And Now...

Without any further delay, turn the page and begin learning to master the Borland C++ 4 language.

Chapter 1

The Borland C++ 4 IDE

C++ History and Basics

C++ was developed by Bjarne Stroustrup, at Bell Labs, the birthplace of C. Stroustrup developed C++ mainly as an object-oriented extension of C. Consequently, C++ shares much of its language syntax, keywords, and libraries with C. This approach enables C programmers to gradually move on to C++ without abandoning the C-based tools and utilities that they either developed or purchased.

The C++ language continues to evolve. Today, the evolution of C++ has moved from the hands of Bell Labs to the ANSI C++ committee. This committee is working to standardize the C++ language and its main libraries.

Although C++ offers new object-oriented constructs to C programmers, some minor non-OOP differences exist between the two languages. These minor differences are found in the area of dynamic allocation (creating variables at runtime) and the declaration of user-defined types (records or structures that logically group data fields to make up a more coherent piece of information—a good example is a user-defined type that stores mailing addresses). C++ regards the tag names of user-defined types as type names. Another area of difference between C and C++ is I/O. Stroustrup introduced a new C++ mechanism that makes input and output more extendable than the C-style I/O, which is also available in C++. Although many C++ programmers use the STDIO.H for C-style I/O, many other C++ programmers recommend the sole use of the C++ stream I/O libraries.

In this chapter, you learn about the following topics:

- The history of C++

- The Borland C++ 4 IDE

- The **File** menu

- The **Edit** menu

- The **Search** menu

- The **View** menu

- The **Project** menu

- The **Debug** menu

- The **Tool** menu

- The **Options** menu

- The **Window** menu

- The **Help** menu

The Borland C++ 4 IDE

The Borland C++ IDE is an MDI-compliant window with the following main components:

- The *window frame* with the menu system, minimize, and maximize icons. You can resize, move, maximize, and minimize the Borland C++ IDE window. This window has a title that reflects the name of the active window.

- The *menu system,* which offers numerous options.

- The *speed bar,* which contains special bitmapped buttons that offer shortcuts to specific commands. The IDE enables you to customize the bitmapped buttons in the speed bar. In addition, these buttons are context-sensitive. Their number and type change, depending on the current task or active window. The IDE supports a nice feature that displays text in the status line to describe a bitmapped button's action when you move the mouse over that button.

- The *client area,* which contains various windows, such as the source code editing window, the message window, the variable watch window, and so on.

- The *status line* located at the bottom of the IDE window. This line displays brief on-line help as you move the mouse over the buttons in the speed bar. The status line also offers a brief explanation for the various menu items, displays the cursor location, and shows the status of the insert/overwrite mode.

Figure 1.1 shows a sample session with the Borland C++ IDE.

The File Menu

The File menu provides options to open files, save files, print text, and exit the IDE. Table 1.1 summarizes the options in the File menu. The File menu also includes a dynamic list of the most recently opened source code files.

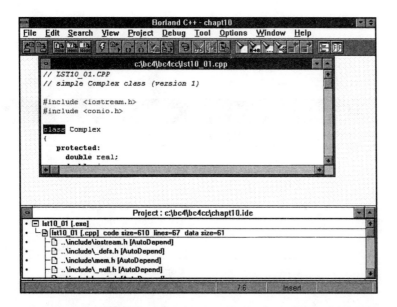

Figure 1.1
The Borland C++
IDE.

Table 1.1. A summary of the options in the File menu.

Command	Shortcut Key(s)	Function
New		Opens a new edit window
Open		Loads an existing source code file into a new edit window
Save	Ctrl+K s	Saves the contents of the active edit window
Save **A**s		Saves the contents of the active edit window using a new filename
Save A**ll**		Saves all of the opened source code windows in their respective files
Print		Prints the contents of a source code window
Print Setup		Sets up the printer
E**x**it		Exits the IDE

The Edit Menu

The Edit menu contains options that enable you to edit the text in the edit windows. Table 1.2 summarizes the options in the Edit menu.

Table 1.2. A summary of the options in the Edit menu.		
Command	**Shortcut Key(s)**	**Function**
Undo	Ctrl+Z	Undoes the last editing action
Redo	Shift+Ctrl+Z	Reverses the action of the last Undo option
Cu**t**	Ctrl+X	Deletes the selected text and copies it in the Clipboard (erases the previous contents of the Clipboard)
Copy	Ctrl+C	Copies the selected text to the Clipboard (erases the previous contents of the Clipboard)
Paste	Ctrl+V	Inserts the contents of the Clipboard at the current cursor location
Cl**e**ar	Ctrl+Delete	Deletes selected text but does not write it to the Clipboard
Select all		Selects all of the text in the active edit window
Bu**f**fer List		Displays the Buffer List dialog box

The Search Menu

The Search menu contains options that enable you to locate various kinds of information, such as text, symbol definitions, function declarations, and program building errors. Table 1.3 offers a summary of the options in the Search menu.

Table 1.3. A summary of the options in the Search menu.		
Command	**Shortcut Key(s)**	**Function**
Find	Ctrl+Q f	Searches for text in the active edit window
Replace	Ctrl+Q a	Replaces text in the active source code window

Command	Shortcut Key(s)	Function
Search Again	F3	Repeats the last Find or Replace operation
Browse Symbol		Locates a symbol in any source code that is part of the current project
Locate Function		Locates a function
Previous Message	Alt+F7	Selects the previous program building message and places the cursor at the offending line in an edit window
Next Message	Alt+F8	Selects the next program building message and places the cursor at the offending line in an edit window

The **V**iew Menu

The **V**iew menu contains options that empower you to view and browse a wide variety of information. This information goes beyond the declarations in the source code files of your own project. Table 1.4 contains a summary of the options in the **V**iew menu.

Table 1.4. A summary of the options in the View menu.		
Command	**Shortcut Key(s)**	**Function**
ClassExpert		Invokes the ClassExpert utility that works with project files generated by AppExpert
Project		Displays the Project window
Message		Displays the Message window
Classes		Browses through the classes
Globals		Browses through global data types, constants, and variables
Watch		Selects or opens the Watch window
Breakpoint		Selects or opens the Breakpoints window
Call **S**tack		Selects or opens the Call Stack window
Register		Selects or opens the Registers window

(continues)

Table 1.4. Continued		
Command	**Shortcut Key(s)**	**Function**
Event Log		Selects or opens the Event Log window
Information		Displays compiler information

The Project Menu

The **P**roject menu offers options with which you manage a project to build an executable program or a library. Table 1.5 contains a summary of the options in the **P**roject menu.

Table 1.5. A summary of the options in the Project menu.		
Command	**Shortcut Key(s)**	**Function**
AppExpert		Invokes the AppExpert utility to generate the files of a project
New Project		Creates a new project
Open Project		Opens an existing project and closes the current project
Close Project		Closes the current project
New Target		Creates a new target in the current project
Compile	Alt+F9	Compiles the file in the active edit window
Make All		Updates the project files by compiling and linking the necessary source code files
Build All		Unconditionally compiles and links all of the project source code files
Generate Makefile		Generates a .MAK makefile

The Debug Menu

The **D**ebug menu provides you with options that enable you to manage debugging your C or C++ source code. Table 1.6 presents a summary of the options in the **D**ebug menu.

Table 1.6. A summary of the options in the Debug menu.

Command	Shortcut Key(s)	Function
Run	Ctrl+F9	Runs the program of the current target; when necessary, this option also compiles and links the project source code files
Step Over	F8	Single-steps through the next statement without tracing the statements of functions called in the next statement
Trace Into	F7	Single-steps through the next statement and traces the statements of functions called in the next statement
Toggle Brea**k**point	F5	Toggles making the line at the breakpoint current cursor location an unconditional breakpoint
Find Execution		Shows the source code at the point of execution
Pause Program		Pauses the program and switches to the debugger
Terminate Pro**g**ram	Ctrl+F2	Stops the program and restarts it from the beginning
Add **W**atch	Ctrl+F5	Opens the Watch Properties dialog box to add a variable to watch
Add **B**reakpoint		Opens the Breakpoint Properties dialog box to add a breakpoint
Evaluate/Modify		Evaluates an expression and/or modifies the value in a variable
Inspect	Alt+F5	Inspects the contents of a variable
Load Symbol Table		Loads DLL symbol table

The T̲ool Menu

The **T**ool menu provides you with the access to several programming utilities. The IDE **T**ools option in the **O**ptions menu enables you to customize the list of programming tools that appear in the **T**ool menu. Table 1.7 provides you with a summary of the default options in the **T**ool menu.

Chapter 11, "Advanced Object-Oriented Programming," discusses some of the Windows programming tools.

Table 1.7. A summary of the default options in the Tool menu.

Command	Shortcut Key(s)	Function
TDW		Invokes the Turbo Debugger for Windows to work with the current target node
Resource Workshop		Invokes the Resource Workshop utility
Grep		Runs the Grep utility on the currently selected nodes
WinSight		Invokes the WinSight utility to monitor Windows messages
W**I**nSpector		Runs the WinSpector utility to perform post-mortem analysis
Key Map Compiler		Compiles the IDE key map file

The **O**ptions Menu

The **O**ptions menu enables you to fine-tune the operations of the compiler, linker, editor, and all of the other components of the IDE. Table 1.8 shows the summary of the options in the **O**ptions menu.

Table 1.8. A summary of the options in the Options menu.

Command	Shortcut Key(s)	Function
Project		Inspects and edits the setting of the current project
Environment		Views and edits the setting of the environment
Tools		Adds and/or deletes tools in the Tool commands
Sty**l**e Sheets		Edits the options style sheets
Save		Configures to save the project, desktop, and environment

The <u>W</u>indow Menu

The **W**indow menu offers options to manage windows in the IDE client area. These options enable you to arrange, close, minimize, and restore some or all windows. In addition to the standard options, the **W**indow menu also lists the current windows. Table 1.9 summarizes the **W**indow menu options.

Command	Shortcut Key(s)	Function
Table 1.9. A summary of the options in the Window menu.		
Cascade	Shift+F5	Cascades the windows in the client area of the IDE
Tile **H**orizontal	Shift+F4	Tiles the windows horizontally on client area of the IDE
Tile Vertical		Tiles the windows vertically on client area of the IDE
Arrange **I**cons		Arranges the icons in the client area of the IDE
Close **A**ll		Closes all windows, debugger windows, browser windows, or editor windows
Mi**n**imize All		Minimizes all windows, debugger windows, browser windows, or editor windows
Restore All		Restores all windows, debugger windows, browser windows, or editor windows

The <u>H</u>elp Menu

The **H**elp menu provides you with the kind of on-line help that is familiar to most users of Windows programs. Table 1.10 shows a summary of the options in the **H**elp menu.

Command	Shortcut Key(s)	Function
Table 1.10. A summary of the options in the Help menu.		
Contents		Displays the table of contents for the on-line help system

(continues)

Table 1.10. Continued

Command	Shortcut Key(s)	Function
Keyword Search	F1	Displays help regarding the keyword where the current cursor is located
Keyboard		Displays information that explains the mapping of the keyboard
Using Help		Displays information to assist you in using the on-line help system
About		Displays information regarding the software version and copyright

Summary

This chapter presented a brief history of C++ and discussed the menu options and selections of the Borland C++ 4 IDE. The chapter offered the following information:

- C++ extends the C language mainly in the area of object-oriented programming.

- The File menu manages files and directory operations, and exits the IDE.

- The Edit menu performs Clipboard operations and undoes the preceding edit changes. The Clipboard operations include Cut, Copy, and Paste.

- The Search menu searches for and replaces text, locates functions, and indicates error locations in a file.

- The View menu enables you to view and browse through various kinds of information, such as the declarations of functions, data types, and messages.

- The Project menu compiles, links, builds, and makes programs.

- The Debug menu manages the aspects of debugging a program. The selections in this menu enable you to set and clear breakpoints and watch variables.

■ The **P**roject menu manages project files that enable you to compile an application made up of multiple source code files.

■ The **O**ptions menu views and alters the various default settings of Borland C++ 4. Among the options are those related to the compiler, the linker, colors, editors, directories, and the mouse.

■ The **T**ool menu enables you to invoke various programming tools, such as the Turbo Debugger, the Resource Workshop, the WinSpector utility, and the WinSight utility.

■ The **O**ptions menu empowers you to fine tune various aspects of the IDE such as the editor, compiler, and linker.

■ The **W**indows menu manages displaying, closing, and arranging the various windows.

■ The **H**elp menu provides powerful on-line help.

Chapter 2

Getting Started

A Simple C++ Program

If you have ever programmed in another language, the first C++ program in this chapter may seem like a walk down memory lane. This simple program displays a one-line greeting message. This program enables you to see the very basic components of a C++ program.

Listing 2.1 contains the source code for program LST02_01.CPP, which displays the string "Hello, Programmer!".

Listing 2.1. The source code for the LST02_01.CPP program.

```
// LST02_01.CPP
// A trivial C++ program that says hello

#include <iostream.h>

main()
{
  cout << "Hello, Programmer!";
  return 0;
}
```

Examine the code in the preceding program. Notice the following characteristics of a C++ program:

- The comments in C++ use the // characters for comments that run to the end of the line. C++ also supports the C-style comments that begin with the /* characters and end with the */ characters.

- The C++ program supports two levels of code: global and functions (C++ functions cannot contain nested functions). The function main()

Your journey in the world of C++ begins in this chapter, which presents the following basic topics:

- Getting started with C++

- The various compiler directives

plays an important role, because program execution begins with this function. Therefore, a C++ program can have only a single `main()` function. You can place the `main()` function anywhere in the code. Because `main()` is a function similar to any other C++ function, it can have its own local data types, constants, and variables. Further, the `main()` function should return a value, just like any other function.

■ C++ strings are enclosed in double quotation marks, and characters are enclosed in single quotation marks. Thus, `'A'` is a character, whereas `"A"` is a single-character string. C++ handles `'A'` and `"A"` differently.

■ C++ uses the { and } characters to define blocks.

■ Every statement in a C++ program ends with a semicolon.

■ This C++ program contains an `#include` compiler directive that instructs the Borland C++ compiler to include the IOSTREAM.H header file. Header files offer a central resource for definitions and declarations used by your program. The IOSTREAM.H provides the operations that support basic stream input and output.

■ The C++ program outputs the string `"Hello, Programmer!"` to the standard output stream, `cout`, which in most cases is the screen. In addition, the program uses the extractor operator, `<<`, to send the emitted string to the output stream.

■ The `main()` function must return a value that reflects the error status of the C++ program. Returning the value `0` signals to the operating system that the program terminated normally.

Compiler Directives

C++ supports various compiler directives, including `#define`, `#undef`, `#include`, `#error`, `#if` (and other related directives), `#line`, and `#pragma`. The following sections cover these directives.

The *#define* Directive

The preprocessor examines your C++ source code to locate the `#define` macro directive. The `#define` directive is a tool for defining constants and pseudofunctions.

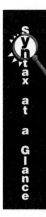

The *#define* Directive
The syntax of the #define directive is

```
#define macro macro_text_or_value
#define macro(parameter_list) macro_expression
```

The *macro_text_or_value* represents the text or value that replaces the macro. The *parameter_list* is a list of parameters that can give a macro great flexibility in generating different results.

Example:
```
#define GRAVITY 9.81
#define ABS(x) ((x) < 0) ? (-x) : (x)
```

The first form of the #define directive defines a macro-based constant. The second form reveals that you can include parameters with the macro. This feature makes macros very flexible. C++ requires that a line contain no more than one #define directive. If you cannot contain the macro expression in one line, you can use the \ character (with a leading space) as a line-continuation code. Macros that possess parameters enable you to create *pseudofunctions*—macro-based functions that are faster than normal functions but require more code space. The additional code space is necessary because the preprocessor substitutes every occurrence of these macros with their respective expressions.

The #define directive serves the following purposes:

- Defines constants

- Replaces reserved words or symbols with others

- Creates pseudo data type identifiers using standard data types

- Creates shorthand commands

- Defines macro-based pseudofunctions

The *#undef* Directive
The counterpart of the #define directive is #undef. This directive undefines a macro. The #undef macro enables you to erase the names of unnecessary

macros. Erasing these macros reclaims the space they occupy and reduces the possibility of conflict with other data items that have the same names.

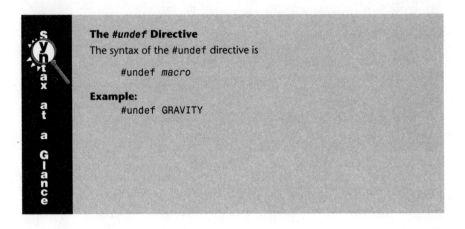

The *#undef* Directive
The syntax of the #undef directive is

    #undef *macro*

Example:
    #undef GRAVITY

C++ enables you to reuse a macro name by placing it in another #define directive. You need not use the #undef directive to explicitly clear a macro definition between two #define directives.

The *#include* Directive

The #include directive enables you to include the source lines from another file into the current one, as though you typed in the included file.

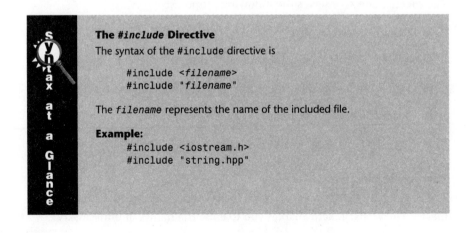

The *#include* Directive
The syntax of the #include directive is

        #include <*filename*>
        #include "*filename*"

The *filename* represents the name of the included file.

Example:
        #include <iostream.h>
        #include "string.hpp"

The two forms of the #include directive differ in how they search for the included file. The first form searches for the file in the special directory for included files, as specified in the IDE Directories topic in the Project command of the Options menu. The second form expands the search to include the current directory.

The *#error* Directive

The #error directive generates an error message. This directive is useful, for example, to signal errors such as incompatible versions.

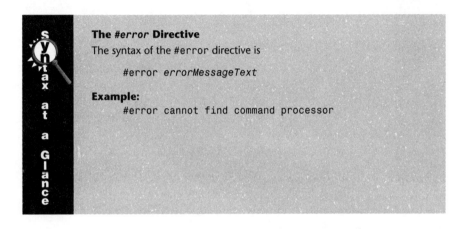

The *#error* Directive
The syntax of the #error directive is

```
#error errorMessageText
```

Example:
```
#error cannot find command processor
```

The preceding directive may yield an error message similar to the following:

```
Error: filename line 19 : Error directive : cannot find command processor
```

The Conditional Compilation Directives

The #if directive enables you to perform conditional compilation of your C++ program. Turbo C++ provides the #if, #elif, #else, and #endif directives to support conditional compilation.

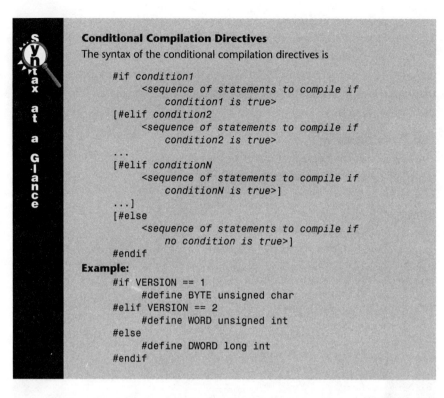

Conditional Compilation Directives

The syntax of the conditional compilation directives is

```
#if condition1
      <sequence of statements to compile if
          condition1 is true>
[#elif condition2
      <sequence of statements to compile if
          condition2 is true>
...
[#elif conditionN
      <sequence of statements to compile if
          conditionN is true>]
...]
[#else
      <sequence of statements to compile if
          no condition is true>]
#endif
```

Example:

```
#if VERSION == 1
      #define BYTE unsigned char
#elif VERSION == 2
      #define WORD unsigned int
#else
      #define DWORD long int
#endif
```

The conditional compilation directives are very useful in compiling specific statements when conditions are either true or false. These directives enable you to have multiple versions of a program that reside in the same source file. You can generate each version of a program by defining certain macros that are associated with each version.

The *#ifdef* and *#ifndef* Directives

C++ provides additional conditional compilation directives. The #ifdef directive compiles a set of lines if a macro *is* defined. The #ifndef directive compiles a set of lines if a macro *is not* defined.

The *#ifdef* and *#ifndef* Conditional Compilation Directives

The syntaxes of these conditional compilation directives are

```
#ifdef macroName
    <sequence of statements to compile if
        macroName is defined>
#endif

#ifndef macroName
    <sequence of statements to compile if
        macroName is not defined>
#endif
```

Examples:
```
#ifdef HAS_BYTE
    #define BYTE unsigned char
#endif

#ifndef HAS_BYTE
    #define WORD unsigned int
#endif
```

The *#line* Directive

The #line directive enables you to specify the line number to a program for cross-referencing or reporting an error either in the preprocessor or for compilation purposes. This directive is especially useful in working with a large number of modules.

The *#line* Directive

The syntax of the #line directive is

```
#line number ["filename"]
```

Example:
```
#line 12 "string.cpp"
```

The #line directive enables you to specify the location of the line number in the original file rather than the location of the line in the preprocessed file. The latter may vary if you include other files—a likely event. The *filename* clause is necessary only the first time you use the #line directive.

The *#pragma* Directive

The #pragma directive supports implementation-specific directives without affecting other implementations of C++. If a C++ compiler does not support a specific pragma directive, the compiler ignores that directive.

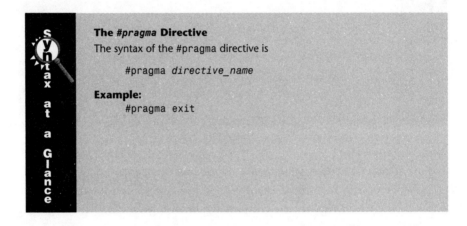

The *#pragma* Directive
The syntax of the #pragma directive is

```
#pragma directive_name
```

Example:
```
#pragma exit
```

The Borland C++ 4 compiler has the following #pragma directives:

■ The #pragma startup statement instructs the compiler to execute a specific function *before* the main() function when you start a program. The syntax of this directive is

```
#pragma startup function [priority]
```

The optional *priority* parameter is an integer in the range of 64 to 255. When this parameter is omitted, the compiler assigns the default value of 100. The lower values have a higher priority. Using the priorities with the #pragma startup, you can specify multiple startup functions and the order of their execution before calling function main().

■ The #pragma exit directive specifies the function that is called *after* the main() function when you end a program. The syntax of this directive is

```
#pragma exit function [priority]
```

The *priority* parameter (similar to the one used in #pragma startup) specifies the order of execution for those functions that follow the function main().

■ The #pragma hdrfile directive specifies the name of the file that stores the precompiled headers. Precompiled headers speed up recompiling a program, because the header files are compiled once and need not be recompiled. The default name for the file that stores the precompiled headers is TCDEF.SYM. The syntax of this directive is

```
#pragma hdrfile "filename.SYM"
```

■ The #pragma hdrstop directive ends the list of files that are eligible for precompilation.

■ The #pragma inline directive tells the compiler that the source code includes inline assembly language statements.

■ The #pragma option directive enables you to specify command-line options in your source code. The syntax of this directive is

```
#pragma option [options...]
```

For example, the directive

```
#pragma option -Dversion=1.0
```

defines the identifier version and assigns it the string 1.0.

■ The #pragma saveregs directive ensures that a huge function does not alter the values of any of the CPU registers when it is called. Such functions normally use additional CPU registers to handle the address segment and offset. Consequently, you may lose valuable information in the additional CPU registers. The #pragma saveregs directive protects you from such loss.

■ The #pragma warn directive enables you to check the Display Warning settings (in the Messages Options dialog box) or override the -wxxx warning command-line option. The syntax of the #pragma warn directive is

```
#pragma warn [+ ¦ - ¦ .]xxx
```

The + symbol turns on the warn pragma. The - symbol turns off the warn pragma. The dot symbol restores the warn pragma to the value it had when the file compilation started.

■ The #pragma argused directive is permitted strictly between function definitions and affects only the next function. This directive disables the warning message which indicates that a certain parameter is never used in a function. The syntax of this #pragma directive is

```
#pragma argused
```

■ The #pragma codeseg enables you to name the segment, class, or group that contains functions. The syntax of this #pragma directive is

```
#pragma codeseg <seg_name> <"seg_class"> <group>
```

■ The #pragma comment enables you to write a comment record into an .OBJ file. You can use the comment directive to specify the name of a library module that is not specified in the response file of the linker. The syntax of this #pragma directive is

```
#pragma comment(LIB, "lib_module_name")
```

For example the following pragma includes the MYCALC.LIB file in creating an .OBJ file:

```
#pragma comment(LIB, mycalc.lib)
```

■ The #pragma intrinsic empowers you to override IDE options or command-line switches that control the inlining of functions. The syntax of this #pragma directive is

```
#pragma intrinsic [-]function_name
```

The following intrinsic pragma, for example, prevents the compiler from generating an inline code for function strlen():

```
#program intrinsic -strlen
```

Summary

In this chapter, you began learning how to use C++. You learned about the following topics:

■ The basic components of a C++ program. These include comments, the main() function, and the declaration of simple variables.

■ Turbo C++'s support of the following directives:

   ■ The #define directive, that you use to define macros.

   ■ The #undef directive, with which you can undefine a macro.

   ■ The #include directive, which enables you to include files to be compiled with the currently compiled source file.

   ■ The #error directive, that generates an error message.

   ■ The conditional compilation directives, which enable you to perform conditional compilation of your C++ program.

   ■ The #line directive, with which you can specify the line number to a program for cross-referencing or reporting an error.

   ■ The #pragma directive, that supports implementation-specific directives.

Chapter 3

Variables and Operators

Predefined Data Types

C++ offers the `int`, `char`, `float`, `double`, and `void` data types. The `void` data type is a special valueless type. C++ adds more flexibility to data types by supporting what are known as *data type modifiers*. These modifiers alter the precision and the range of values. The type modifiers are `signed`, `unsigned`, `short`, and `long`.

Constants

C++ offers constants in two flavors: macro-based and formal. The macro-based constants are inherited from C and use the `#define` compiler directive (this directive is covered in chapter 2, "Getting Started"). The second type of constant in C++ is the formal constant.

The Formal Constant
The syntax of the formal constant is

```
const dataType constantName = constantValue;
```

The *dataType* item is an optional item that specifies the data type of the constant values. If you omit the data type, the C++ compiler assumes the `int` type.

Examples:
```
const unsigned daysInWeek = 7;
const hoursPerDay = 24;
```

This chapter discusses:

- Predefined data types

- Constants and variables

- Arithmetic operators

- Increment and decrement operators

- Assignment operators

- The `sizeof` operator

- Typecasting

- Relational and logical operators

- Bit-manipulation operators

- The comma operator

> **Caution**
>
> Many C++ programmers, including the gurus behind C++, advise against using the #define directive to define constants. They favor the formal constants, because these enable the compiler to perform type checking.

Variables

Variables and other identifiers in C++ are case-sensitive. The name of a variable must begin with a letter and can contain other letters, digits, and the underscore character. The names of variables in Borland C++ 4 are significant to any length. When you declare a variable in a program, you must associate a data type with it. C++ enables you to assign a value to variables when you declare them.

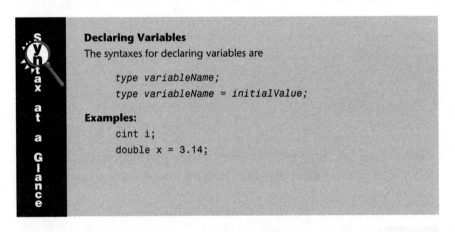

Declaring Variables
The syntaxes for declaring variables are

```
type variableName;
type variableName = initialValue;
```

Examples:
```
cint i;
double x = 3.14;
```

C++ enables you to declare in a declaration statement a list of variables that have the same types. For example:

```
int j, i = 2, k = 3;
double x = 3.12;
double y = 2 * x, z = 4.5, a = 45.7;
```

The initializing values can include other previously defined variables or constants.

Arithmetic Operators

Table 3.1 shows the C++ operators. The compiler performs floating-point or integer division, depending on the operands. If both operands are integer expressions, the compiler produces the code for an integer division. If either operand or both operands are floating-point expressions, the compiler yields code for floating-point division.

C++ Operator	Purpose	Data Type	Example
+	Unary plus	Numeric	`x = +y + 3;`
-	Unary minus	Numeric	`x = -y;`
+	Add	Numeric	`z = y + x;`
-	Subtract	Numeric	`z = y - x;`
*	Multiply	Numeric	`z = y * x;`
/	Divide	Numeric	`z = y / x;`
%	Modulus	Integer	`z = y % x;`

Table 3.1. The C++ arithmetic operators.

The Increment and Decrement Operators

C++ provides special increment and decrement operators, ++ and −. These operators enable you to increment and decrement by one the value stored in a variable.

Increment Operators

The syntaxes of the increment operators are

```
variable++  // post-increment
++variable  // pre-increment
```

Examples:
```
dayNumber++;
dayArray[++dayNumber];
```

Decrement Operators

The syntaxes of the decrement operators are

```
variable --  // post-decrement
--variable   // pre-decrement
```

Examples:
```
dayNumber--;
dayArray[--dayNumber];
```

The syntaxes of these operators indicate that you can apply the ++ and -- operators two ways. Placing these operators to the left of their operands alters the value of the operand *before* the operand contributes its value in an expression. Similarly, placing these operators to the right of their operands changes the value of the operand *after* the operand contributes its value in an expression. If the ++ or -- operators are the only operators in a statement, the pre- and post-forms perform identically.

Here are a few simple examples:

```
int i, j, k = 5;
k++; // k is now 6, same effect as ++k
--k; // k is now 5, same effect as k--
k = 5;
i = 4 * k++; // k is now 6 and i is 20
k = 5;
j = 4 * ++k; // k is now 6 and j is 24
```

The first statement uses the post-increment ++ operator to increment the value of variable k. If you write ++k instead, you get the same result when the statement finishes executing. The second statement uses the pre-decrement -- operator. Again, writing k-- instead, produces the same result. The next two statements assign 5 to variable k and then use the post-increment ++ operator in a simple math expression. This statement multiplies 4 by the current value of k (that is, 5), assigns the result of 20 to the variable i, and then increments the values in variable k to 6. The last two statements show a different outcome. The last statement first increments the value in variable k (the value in variable k becomes 6), performs the multiplication, and then assigns the result of 24 to the variable j.

The Assignment Operators

As a programmer, you often come across statements similar to these:

```
IndexOfFirstElement = IndexOfFirstElement + 4;
GraphicsScaleRatio = GraphicsScaleRatio * 3;
CurrentRateOfReturn = CurrentRateOfReturn / 4;
DOSfileListSize = DOSfileListSize - 10;
IndexOfLastElement = IndexOfLastElement % 23;
```

The variable that receives the result of an expression is also the first operand. (Of course, because the addition and multiplication are communicative operations, the assigned variable can be either operand with these operations.)

Notice that the preceding expression shows the same variable names on both sides of the equal sign. Using long descriptive names, as in this expression, requires more typing and, therefore, is more prone to errors. The preceding examples are slightly exaggerated to show the value of the assignment operators that follow.

C++ offers assignment operators that combine simple math operators and the assignment operator. For example, you can write the following statements:

```
IndexOfFirstElement += 4;
GraphicsScaleRatio *= 3;
CurrentRateOfReturn /= 4;
DOSfileListSize -= 10;
IndexOfLastElement %= 23;
```

Notice that the name of the variable appears only once. Also notice that the statements use the operators +=, *=, /=, -=, and %=. Table 3.2 shows these arithmetic assignment operators. C++ supports other types of assignment operators as well (see table 3.5).

Table 3.2. The arithmetic assignment operators.		
Operator	**Long Form**	**Short Form**
+=	x = x + y;	x + = 12;
-=	x = x - y;	x - = y;
*=	x = x * y;	x * = y;
/=	x = x / y;	x / = y;
%=	x = x % y;	x % = y;

The *sizeof* Operator

Often your programs need to know the byte size of a data type or variable. C++ provides the `sizeof` operator, which takes for an argument either a data type or the name of a variable (`scalar`, `array`, `record`, and so on).

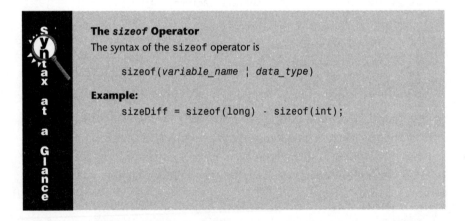

The *sizeof* Operator
The syntax of the sizeof operator is

```
sizeof(variable_name | data_type)
```

Example:
```
sizeDiff = sizeof(long) - sizeof(int);
```

Typecasting

Automatic data conversion is one of the duties of a compiler. This data conversion simplifies expressions and relieves the frustration of both novice and veteran programmers. With behind-the-scenes data conversion, you need not study each expression that mixes somewhat similar data types in your program. For example, the compiler handles most expressions that mix various types of integers or that mix integers and floating-point types. You get a compile-time error if you try to do something illegal!

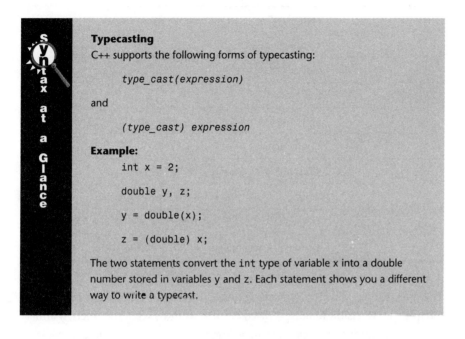

Typecasting

C++ supports the following forms of typecasting:

```
type_cast(expression)
```

and

```
(type_cast) expression
```

Example:

```
int x = 2;

double y, z;

y = double(x);

z = (double) x;
```

The two statements convert the int type of variable x into a double number stored in variables y and z. Each statement shows you a different way to write a typecast.

Relational and Logical Operators

The relational and logical operators are the basic building blocks of decision-making constructs in any programming language. Table 3.3 shows the C++ relational and logical operators. Notice that C++ does not spell out the operators AND, OR, and NOT; instead, it uses single- and dual-character symbols. Also notice that C++ does not support the relational XOR (exclusive OR) operator. You can use the following #define macro directives to define the AND, OR, and NOT identifiers as macros if you prefer to use descriptive symbols rather than the cryptic single- and dual-character symbols:

```
#define AND &&
#define OR ¦¦
#define NOT !
```

Although these macros are permissible in C++, you are likely to get a negative reaction from veteran C++ programmers who read them in your code.

Table 3.3. The C++ relational and logical operators.

Operator	Meaning	Example
&&	Logical AND	`a && b`
¦¦	Logical OR	`c ¦¦ d`
!	Logical NOT	`!c`
<	Less than	`i < 0`
<=	Less than or equal to	`i <= 0`
>	Greater than	`j > 10`
>=	Greater than or equal to	`x >= 8.2`
==	Equal to	`c == '\0'`
!=	Not equal to	`c != '\n'`
?:	Conditional assignment	`k = (i<1) ? 1 : i;`

The operators in table 3.3 typically are used by decision-making constructs (chapter 5, "Decision Making," discusses the `if` and `switch` statements) and by loops (chapter 6, "Loops," discusses the `for`, `do-while`, and `while` loops).

In table 3.3, you may notice the last operator, `?:`. This special operator supports what is known as the *conditional expression*. The conditional expression is shorthand for a dual-alternative simple `if-else` statement (more about the `if` statement in chapter 5, "Decision Making"):

```
if (condition)
     variable = expression1;
else
     variable = expression2;
```

The equivalent conditional expression is

```
variable = (condition) ? expression1 : expression2;
```

The conditional expression tests the condition. If that condition is true, it assigns *expression1* to the target variable; otherwise, it assigns *expression2* to the target variable.

Caution

Do not make the mistake of using the = operator as the equality relational operator. This common mistake is a source of logical bugs in a C++ program. You may be accustomed to using the = operator in other languages for testing the equality of two data items. In C++, you must use the == operator. So what happens if you employ the = operator in C++? You *may* get a compiler warning. Other than that, your C++ program should run; a session with such a program, however, is likely to lead to bizarre program behavior or even a system hang! When the program reaches the expression that is supposed to test for equality, it actually attempts to assign the operand on the right of the = sign to the operand on the left of the = sign. Here is an example:

```
int i = 10;
int j = 20;
int areEqual;
areEqual = (i = j);
```

The last statement assigns the value of variable j to variable i and then to variable areEqual. As the name of the areEqual variable suggests, the intent of the code writer is to assign the result of the relational expression that compares the contents of variables i and j. The correct statement is

```
areEqual = (i == j);
```

Bit-Manipulation Operators

The C++ programming language is suitable for system development. System development requires bit-manipulation operators to toggle, set, query, and shift the bits of a byte or word. Table 3.4 shows the bit-manipulation operators. Notice that C++ uses the symbols & and ¦ to represent the bitwise AND and OR, respectively. Recall that the && and ¦¦ characters represent the *logical* AND and OR operators, respectively. In addition to the bit-manipulation operators, C++ supports the bit-manipulation assignment operators, shown in table 3.5.

Table 3.4. The bit-manipulation operators in C++.		
Operator	**Meaning**	**Example**
&	Bitwise AND	i & 128
¦	Bitwise OR	j ¦ 64
^	Bitwise XOR	j ^ 12
~	Bitwise NOT	~j
<<	Bitwise shift left	i << 2
>>	Bitwise shift right	j >> 3

Table 3.5. The C++ bit-manipulation assignment operators.		
Operator	**Long Form**	**Short Form**
&=	x = x & y;	x &= y;
¦=	x = x ¦ y;	x ¦= y;
^=	x = x ^ y;	x ^= y;
<<=	x = x << y;	x <<= y;
>>=	x = x >> y;	x >>= y;

The Comma Operator

The Comma Operator
The syntax of the comma operator is

```
expression1, expression2
```

Example:
```
a = b = c, c = a;
```

The comma operator requires the program to completely evaluate the first expression before evaluating the second expression. Notice that both expressions are *located in the same C++ statement*. What does "located in the same C++ statement" mean, exactly, and why utilize this rather unusual operator in the first place? These questions have a lot of merit. The comma operator with its peculiar role does serve a specific and very important purpose in the `for` loop. Using the comma operator enables you to create multiple expressions that initialize multiple loop-related variables. You learn more about `for` loop and the comma operator in chapter 6, "Loops."

Now that you have read about most of the C++ operators (chapter 8, "Pointers," discusses a few more operators that deal with pointers and addresses), you need to know about two related aspects: the *precedence* of the C++ operators and the *direction* (or sequence) of evaluation. Table 3.6 shows the C++ precedence of the operators covered so far and indicates the evaluation direction. The precedence values quantify the precedence of the various operators—especially for some operators that are in the same category but have a different precedence. These values are not actually used by the compiler.

Table 3.6. The C++ operators and their precedence.

Name	Symbol	Eval. Direction	Precedence
Unary			
Post-increment	++	Left to right	2
Post-decrement	--	Left to right	2
Address	&	Right to left	2
Bitwise NOT	~	Right to left	2
Typecast	(*type*)	Right to left	2
Logical NOT	!	Right to left	2
Negation	-	Right to left	2
Plus sign	+	Right to left	2
Pre-increment	++	Right to left	2
Pre-decrement	--	Right to left	2
Size of data	sizeof	Right to left	2

(continues)

Table 3.6. Continued			
Name	**Symbol**	**Eval. Direction**	**Precedence**
Multiplicative			
Modulus	%	Left to right	3
Multiply	*	Left to right	3
Divide	/	Left to right	3
Additive			
Add	+	Left to right	4
Subtract	-	Left to right	4
Bitwise Shift			
Shift left	<<	Left to right	5
Shift right	>>	Left to right	5
Relational			
Less than	<	Left to right	6
Less or equal	<=	Left to right	6
Greater than	>	Left to right	6
Greater or equal	>=	Left to right	6
Equal to	==	Left to right	7
Not equal to	!=	Left to right	7
Bitwise			
AND	&	Left to right	8
XOR	^	Left to right	9
OR	¦	Left to right	10
Logical			
AND	&&	Left to right	11
OR	¦¦	Left to right	12

Name	Symbol	Eval. Direction	Precedence
Ternary			
Cond. express.	?:	Right to left	13
Assignment			
Arithmetic	=	Right to left	14
	+=	Right to left	14
	-=	Right to left	14
	*=	Right to left	14
	/=	Right to left	14
	%=	Right to left	14
Shift	>>=	Right to left	14
	<<=	Right to left	14
Bitwise	&=	Right to left	14
	¦=	Right to left	14
	^=	Right to left	14
Comma	,	Left to right	15

Summary

This chapter discussed the following topics:

- The predefined data types.

- The two types of constants in C++: the macro-based constants and the formal constants.

- Variables in C++, which must be associated with data types and can be initialized during their declaration.

- The arithmetic operators, including the +, -, *, /, and % (modulus).

■ The increment and decrement operators. These operators come in pre- and post-forms. C++ enables you to apply these operators to variables that store characters, integers, and even floating-point numbers.

■ The arithmetic assignment operators, which enable you to write shorter arithmetic expressions in which the primary operand is also the variable receiving the result of the expression.

■ The sizeof operator, which returns the byte size of either a data type or a variable.

■ Typecasting, which enables you to force the type conversion of an expression.

■ Relational and logical operators that enable you to build logical expressions. C++ does not support a predefined Boolean type and instead considers 0 (zero) as false and any nonzero value as true.

■ The conditional expression, which offers a short form for the simple dual-alternative if-else statement (covered in chapter 5, "Decision Making").

■ The bit-manipulation operators that perform bitwise AND, OR, XOR, and NOT operations. In addition, C++ supports the << and >> bitwise shift operators.

■ The bit-manipulation assignment operators that offer short forms for simple bit-manipulation statements.

■ The comma operator, which is a very special operator. It separates multiple expressions in the same statements and requires the program to completely evaluate one expression before evaluating the next one.

Chapter 4

Managing I/O

Formatted Stream Output

Listing 4.1 shows how to use the standard output stream to create formatted output. The IOSTREAM.H contains functions that specify the width and the number of digits for floating-point numbers.

Listing 4.1. The source code for the LST04_01.CPP program.

```
// LST04_01.CPP
// Program uses C++ stream output.

#include <iostream.h>

main()
{
  short    aShort      = 4;
  int      anInt       = 67;
  unsigned char aByte = 128;
  unsigned aWord       = 65000U;
  long     aLong       = 2000000L;
  char     aChar       = '!';
  float    aSingle     = 355.0;
  double   aDouble      = 1.130e+002;
  // display sample expressions
  cout.width(5); cout << aWord << " - ";
  cout.width(2); cout << aShort << " = ";
  cout.width(5); cout << (aWord - aShort) << '\n';

  cout.width(3); cout << int(aByte) << " + ";
  cout.width(2); cout << anInt << " = ";
  cout.width(3); cout << (aByte + anInt) << '\n';

  cout.width(7); cout << aLong << " / ";
  cout.width(5); cout << aWord << " = ";
  cout.width(3); cout << (aLong / aWord) << '\n';
```

(continues)

C++ does not define I/O operations that are part of the core language. Instead, C++ relies—like its parent language, C—on I/O libraries to provide the needed I/O support. This chapter looks at the basic input and output operations and functions that are supported by the IOSTREAM.H and CONIO.H header files. In this chapter, you learn about the following topics:

- Formatted stream output

- Stream input

- Character I/O functions

- Screen control

- Cursor control

Listing 4.1. Continued

```
    cout.precision(4); cout << aSingle << " / ";
    cout.precision(4); cout << aDouble << " = ";
    cout.precision(5); cout << (aSingle / aDouble) << '\n';

    cout << "The character saved in variable aChar is "
        << aChar << '\n';
    return 0;
}
```

Consider the statements that perform the stream output. The program in listing 4.1 uses the stream function width() to specify the output width for the next item displayed by a cout << statement. Notice how many statements are needed to display three integers. In addition, notice that the program uses the expression int(aByte) to typecast the unsigned char type into an int. Without this type conversion, the contents of variable aByte appear as a character. If you use the stream output to display integers that have default widths, you can replace the six stream output statements with a single statement.

The last set of stream output statements outputs the floating-point numbers. The program uses the stream function precision() to specify the total number of digits to display. Again, although it takes six C++ statements to output three floating-point numbers, if you use the stream output to display numbers that have default widths, you can replace the six stream output statements with a single statement.

Stream Input

In addition to the standard output stream, C++ offers the standard input stream, cin. This input stream is able to read predefined data types, such as int, unsigned, long, and char. Typically, you use the inserter operator >> to get input for the predefined data types.

Listing 4.2 shows the source code for the program LST04_02.CPP. The program simply multiplies two numbers. The program prompts you to enter the numbers to multiply. You must delimit these two items with a space and must end your input by pressing the Enter key. The program gets your input using the following statement:

```
    cin >> x >> y;
```

This statement gets the values for the variables x and y from the standard input stream cin. The input operation uses the inserter operator >>.

Listing 4.2. The source code for the LST04_02.CPP program.

```
// LST04_02.CPP
// Program·illustrates standard stream input

#include <iostream.h>

main()
{
  double x, y, z;

  cout << "Enter two numbers: ";
  cin >> x >>  y;
  z = x * y;
  cout << x << " * " << y << " = " << z << "\n";
  return 0;
}
```

Character I/O Functions

Borland C++ 4 offers other functions to support character I/O. Some of these functions are prototyped in the header file CONIO.H and may not be portable to other C++ implementations. The Borland C++ character input functions are as follows:

- The getche() function returns a character from the console and echoes that character on-screen. This function is prototyped in the header file CONIO.H.

- The getch() function returns a character from the console but does not echo that input character. This function is also prototyped in the header file CONIO.H.

- The getchar() function returns a character from the console. This function is prototyped in the header file STDIO.H.

The Borland C++ character output functions are as follows:

- The putch() function emits a single character to the console. This function is prototyped in the header file CONIO.H.

- The putchar() function emits a single character to the console. This function is also prototyped in the header file STDIO.H.

The getchar() and putchar() functions work with input and output devices in general and not just the console. Communications ports and the printer are examples of other input and output devices.

 The character input functions need no argument and return an int type that represents the ASCII code of the input character. Why not return a char type? The answer points back to the traditional approach of C that was inherited by C++. The traditional approach draws a very close association between integers and characters (which always are stored using their numeric ASCII code). Therefore, each character input function merely returns a character in its *raw* form—an ASCII code integer. The same logic is applied to the character output functions, which accept an int type rather than a char type.

The program in listing 4.3 puts some of the character I/O functions to work. This simple program prompts you to enter three characters. The program uses the getche() and getch() functions to enter each character. Notice that the call to getch() is followed by a call to putch() to echo the input character on the console. The functions getche() and getch() do not require you to press Enter. Consequently, these functions support fast character input. On the other hand, these functions give you no chance to correct input errors! The program uses the putch() function to emit the three characters you type. Listing 4.3 contains the source code for program LST04_03.CPP.

Listing 4.3. The source code for the LST04_03.CPP program.

```
// LST04_03.CPP
// Program demonstrates character I/O using getche, getch,
// and putch.

#include <iostream.h>
#include <conio.h>

main()
{
    char char1, char2, char3;

    cout << "Type the first character: ";
    char1 = getche();
    cout << "\nEnter a second character: ";
    char2 = getch(); putch(char2);
    cout << "\nEnter a third character : ";
    char3 = getch(); putch(char3);
    cout << "\n\nYou entered ";
    putch(char1);
    putch(char2);
    putch(char3);
    cout << "\n\n";
```

```
    return 0;
}
```

The following is a sample session with the program in listing 4.3:

```
Type the first character: a
Enter a second character: b
Enter a third character : c

You entered abc
```

Screen Control

The CONIO.H header file declares two functions that enable you to clear the screen and clear to the end of a line:

- The function `clrscr()` clears the screen and places the cursor at the top-left corner of the screen. The declaration of function `clrscr()` is

  ```
  void clrscr(void);
  ```

- The function `clreol()` clears to the end of the current line. The declaration of function `clreol()` is

  ```
  void clreol(void);
  ```

Cursor Control

The CONIO.H header file declares three functions that enable you to set and query the location of the cursor on-screen:

- The function `gotoxy()` moves the location of the cursor to a specified location. The declaration of the function `gotoxy()` is

  ```
  void gotoxy(int x, int y);
  ```

  The parameters x and y specify the screen row and column numbers, respectively.

- The functions `wherex()` and `wherey()` return the row and column number of the cursor location, respectively. The declarations of these two functions are

  ```
  int wherey(void);
  int wherex(void);
  ```

The following example illustrates a program that manipulates the cursor using the gotoxy(), wherex(), and wherey() functions. Listing 4.4 shows the source code for the program LST04_04.CPP. The program displays the letter *o* as it moves from the upper-left corner of the screen in the lower-right direction for a few lines. You press a key to make the letter move. To stop the program, press Shift-Q.

Listing 4.4. The source code for the LST04_04.CPP program.

```
// LST04_04.CPP
// Program illustrates cursor control

#include <conio.h>
#include <dos.h>

main()
{
  char c = ' ';

  clrscr();
  while (c != 'Q') {
        if (wherex() >= 79) gotoxy(1, wherey());
        if (wherey() >= 24) gotoxy(wherex(), 1);
        gotoxy(wherex() + 1, wherey() + 1);
        putch('o');
        c = getch();
        gotoxy(wherex() - 1, wherey());
    putch(' ');
  }
  return 0;
}
```

Summary

This chapter examined the basic input and output operations and functions supported by the IOSTREAM.H, STDIO.H, and CONIO.H header files. In this chapter, you learned about the following topics:

- Formatted stream output, which uses the precision and width to provide some basic formatting output.

- Standard stream input, which supports the insert operator >> to get input for the predefined data types in C++.

■ Character I/O functions, which rely on the I/O libraries. Among these libraries is the CONIO.H file, which defines the character input functions `getche()` and `getch()`, as well as the character output function `putch()`.

■ Screen control, which employs the `clrscr()` and `clreol()` functions (declared in file CONIO.H) to clear the screen and to clear to the end of the line.

■ Cursor control, which can be handled by the functions `gotoxy()`, `wherex()`, and `wherey()` (declared in file CONIO.H) to set and query the cursor location.

Chapter 5

Decision Making

The Single-Alternative *if* Statement

The programs you have seen in preceding chapters execute every statement—no exceptions. In this chapter, you learn how to alter program flow using the if statement. C++ offers various forms of the if statement that enable you to select single-, dual-, and multiple-alternative courses of action.

In any programming language, the decision-making constructs enable applications to examine conditions and specify courses of action. Programming languages vary in the features of their decision-making constructs. This chapter looks at the decision-making constructs in C++ and covers the following topics:

- The single-alternative if statement

- The dual-alternative if-else statement

- The multiple-alternative if-else statement

- The multiple-alternative switch statement

C++ uses the open and close braces (the { and } symbols) to define a block of statements. Listing 5.1 shows a program with a single-alternative if statement. The program prompts you to enter a positive number and stores the input in the variable x. If the value in x is greater than or equal to zero, the program displays the square root of x.

Listing 5.1. The source code for the LST05_01.CPP program.

```
// LST05_01.CPP
// Program demonstrates the single-alternative if statement

#include <iostream.h>
#include <conio.h>
#include <math.h>

main()
{
  double x;
  clrscr();
  cout << "Enter a positive number: ";
  cin >> x;
  if (x >= 0)
    cout << "The square root of " << x
         << " is " << sqrt(x) << "\n";
  return 0;
}
```

Here is a sample session with the program in listing 5.1:

```
Enter a positive number: 25
The square root of 25 is 5
```

The Dual-Alternative *if-else* Statement

This form of the if statement offers two routes of action based on the tested condition. The else keyword separates the statements used to execute each alternative.

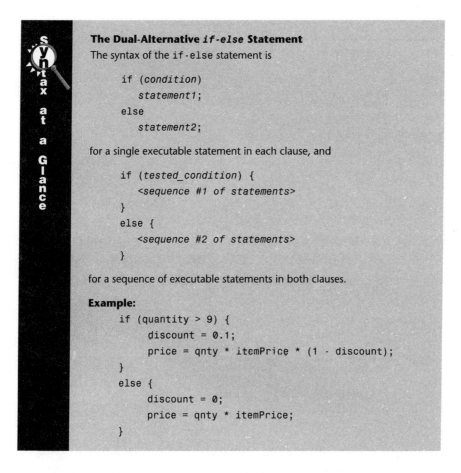

The Dual-Alternative *if-else* Statement

The syntax of the if-else statement is

```
if (condition)
    statement1;
else
    statement2;
```

for a single executable statement in each clause, and

```
if (tested_condition) {
    <sequence #1 of statements>
}
else {
    <sequence #2 of statements>
}
```

for a sequence of executable statements in both clauses.

Example:

```
if (quantity > 9) {
    discount = 0.1;
    price = qnty * itemPrice * (1 - discount);
}
else {
    discount = 0;
    price = qnty * itemPrice;
}
```

Consider the following example that uses the dual-alternative if statement. Listing 5.2 contains the source code for the program LST05_02.CPP. This program prompts you to enter a character and stores your input in the variable c. The program converts your input into uppercase, using the function toupper() (declared in the CTYPE.H header file) and then uses a dual-alternative if statement to determine whether you entered a vowel. The statement in each alternative displays a message confirming whether you entered a vowel.

Listing 5.2. The source code for the LST05_02.CPP program.

```
// LST05_02.CPP
// Program demonstrates the dual-alternative if statement

#include <iostream.h>
#include <conio.h>
#include <ctype.h>

main()
{
  char c;
  clrscr();
  cout << "Enter a character: ";
  cin >> c;
  c = toupper(c);
  if (c == 'A' || c == 'I' || c == 'O' ||
      c == 'E' || c == 'U')
    cout << "You entered a vowel letter\n";
  else
    cout << "You entered a nonvowel letter\n";
  return 0;
}
```

The following is a sample session with the program in listing 5.2:

```
Enter a character: g
You entered a nonvowel letter
```

Potential Problem with the *if* Statements

The dual-alternative if statement presents a potential problem. This problem occurs when the if clause contains another single-alternative if statement. In this case, the compiler thinks that the else clause belongs to the nested if statement. The following code fragment is an example of such a situation:

```
if (i > 0)
    if (i == 10)
        cout << "You guessed the magic number";
else
    cout << "Number is out of range";
```

In this code fragment, when i is a positive number other than 10, the code displays the message Number is out of range. The compiler treats the preceding statements as though the code fragment meant

```
if (i > 0)
    if (i == 10)
        cout << "You guessed the magic number";
    else
        cout << "Number is out of range";
```

To correct this problem, enclose the nested `if` statement in a statement block:

```
if (i > 0) {
    if (i == 10)
        cout << "You guessed the magic number";
}
else
    cout << "Number is out of range";
```

The preceding problem illustrates how the compiler matches the `else` with the closest `if`, unless you use braces to clarify the intent of the `if` statements.

The Multiple-Alternative *if-else* Statement

C++ enables you to nest `if-else` statements to create a multiple-alternative form. This alternative gives your applications a great deal of power and flexibility.

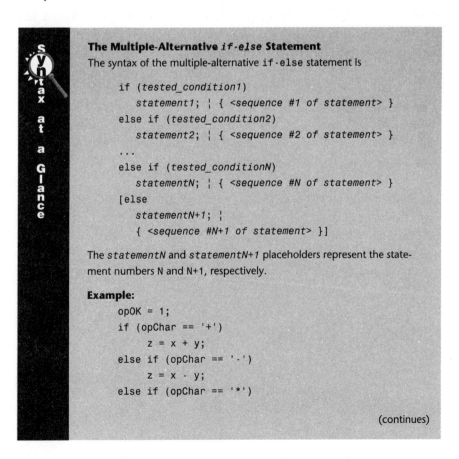

The Multiple-Alternative `if-else` **Statement**
The syntax of the multiple-alternative `if-else` statement Is

```
if (tested_condition1)
    statement1; ¦ { <sequence #1 of statement> }
else if (tested_condition2)
    statement2; ¦ { <sequence #2 of statement> }
...
else if (tested_conditionN)
    statementN; ¦ { <sequence #N of statement> }
[else
    statementN+1; ¦
    { <sequence #N+1 of statement> }]
```

The *statementN* and *statementN+1* placeholders represent the statement numbers N and N+1, respectively.

Example:
```
opOK = 1;
if (opChar == '+')
    z = x + y;
else if (opChar == '-')
    z = x - y;
else if (opChar == '*')
```

(continues)

```
(continued)
        z = x * y;
    else if (opChar == '/' && y != 0)
        z = x / y;
    else
        opOk = 0;
```

The multiple-alternative if-else statement performs a series of cascaded tests until one of the following situations occurs:

- One of the conditions in the if clause or in the else if clauses is true. In this case, the accompanying statements are executed.

- None of the tested conditions is true. The program executes the statements in the catchall else clause (if there is an else clause).

The program in listing 5.3 uses the multiple-alternative if-else statement to determine what type of character is entered. The program identifies the entered character as being one of the following:

- An uppercase letter

- A lowercase letter

- A digit

- A non-alphanumeric character

The program uses an if clause to determine whether the variable c stores an uppercase letter. The program uses two else if clauses to determine whether the variable c contains a lowercase letter or a digit. The catchall else clause detects that variable c does not store an alphanumeric character.

Listing 5.3. The source code for the LST05_03.CPP program.

```
// LST05_03.CPP
// Program demonstrates the multiple-alternative if statement

#include <iostream.h>
#include <conio.h>
#include <ctype.h>

main()
{
  char c;
  clrscr();
  cout << "Enter a character: ";
  cin >> c;
  if (c >= 'A' && c <= 'Z')
    cout << "You entered an uppercase letter\n";
  else if (c >= 'a' && c <= 'z')
    cout << "You entered a lowercase letter\n";
  else if (c >= '0' && c <= '9')
    cout << "You entered a digit\n";
  else
    cout << "You entered a non-alphanumeric character\n";
  return 0;
}
```

Sample output from this program is as follows:

```
Enter a character: !
You entered a non-alphanumeric character
```

The Multiple-Alternative *switch* Statement

The switch statement offers a special form of multiple-alternative decision making. It enables you to examine the various values of an integer-compatible expression and select the appropriate outcome.

The *switch* Statement

The syntax of the switch statement is

```
switch (expression) {
      case constant1_1:
[     case constant1_2: ...]
            <one or more statements>
            break;
      case constant2_1:
[     case constant2_2: ...]
            <one or more statements>
            break;
...
      case constantN_1:
[     case constantN_2: ...]
            <one or more statements>
            break;
      default:
            <one or more statements>
}
```

The general case labels are identified by specifying the alternative number, followed by the underscore and the value number. For example, *constant2_1* stands for the first value in the second alternative of the switch statement.

Example:

```
opOK = 1;
switch (opChar) {
      case '+':
            z = x + y;
            break;
      case '-':
            z = x - y;
            break;
      case '*':
            z = x * y;
            break;
      case '/':
            if (y != 0)
                  z = x / y;
            else
                  opOK = 0;
            break;
      default:
                  opOk = 0;
}
```

The following rules apply to using the `switch` statement:

- The `switch` requires an integer-compatible value. This value can be a constant, a variable, a function call (discussed in more detail in chapter 9, "Functions"), or an expression. The `switch` statement does not work with floating-point data types.

- The value after each `case` label *must be* a constant.

- C++ does not support `case` labels with ranges of values. Instead, each value must appear in a separate `case` label.

- You need to use a `break` statement after each set of executable statements. The `break` statement causes program execution to resume after the end of the current `switch` statement. If you do not use the `break` statement, the program execution resumes at the subsequent `case` labels.

- The `default` clause is a catchall clause.

- The set of statements in each `case` label or grouped `case` label need not be enclosed in open and close braces.

The lack of single `case` labels with ranges of values makes using a multiple-alternative `if-else` statement more appealing if you have a large contiguous range of values.

Listing 5.4 shows a modified version of listing 5.3. The new program performs the same task of classifying your character input but uses a `switch` statement. Notice that the program in this listing includes only a few `case` labels; this arrangement keeps the program listing short. This program is an example of a situation in which using the `if-else` statements is actually more suitable than using the `switch` statement.

Listing 5.4. The source code for the LST05_04.CPP program.

```
// LST05_04.CPP
// Program demonstrates the multiple-alternative
// switch statement

#include <iostream.h>
#include <conio.h>
#include <ctype.h>

main()
```

(continues)

Listing 5.4. Continued

```
{
  char c;
  clrscr();
  cout << "Enter a character: ";
  cin >> c;
  switch (c) {
    case 'A':
    case 'B':
    case 'C':
    // other case labels
      cout << "You entered an uppercase letter\n";
      break;
    case 'a':
    case 'b':
    case 'c':
    // other case labels
      cout << "You entered a lowercase letter\n";
      break;
    case '0':
    case '1':
    case '2':
    // other case labels
      cout << "You entered a digit\n";
      break;
    default:
      cout << "You entered a non-alphanumeric character\n";
  }
  return 0;
}
```

The following lines demonstrate a sample session with the program in listing 5.4:

```
Enter a character: 2
You entered a digit
```

Summary

This chapter presented the various decision-making constructs in C++. These constructs include:

■ The single-, dual-, and multiple-alternative if statements. The if statements require you to observe the following rules:

  ■ You must enclose the tested condition in parentheses.

  ■ You must enclose blocks of statements in pairs of open and close braces.

- The multiple-alternative `switch` statement, which offers a more readable alternative to lengthy `if`/`else if` blocks.

Chapter 6

Loops

The *for* Loop

The for loop in C++ is a versatile loop because it supports fixed as well as conditional iteration. The latter feature of the for loop does not have a parallel in many popular programming languages, such as Pascal and BASIC.

The *for* Loop Statement

The syntax of the for loop statement is

```
for (<initialization of loop control variables>;
    <loop continuation test>;
    <update loop control variables>)
statement; ¦ { <sequence of statements> }
```

Example:
```
for (i = 0; i < 10; i++)
    cout << "The square of " << i << " = "
        << i * i << "\n";
```

Loops are powerful language constructs that enable computers to excel in performing repetitive tasks. This chapter presents the following loops and loop-related topics in C++:

- The for loop statement

- Arrays

- Using for loops to create open loops

- Skipping loop iterations

- Exiting loops

- The do-while loop statement

- The while loop statement

The for loop statement has three components, all optional. The first component initializes the loop control variables (notice the plural, *variables*; C++ enables you to employ more than one loop control variable). The second part of the loop is the condition that determines whether the loop makes another iteration. The last part of the for loop is the clause that increments or decrements the loop control variables.

The C++ for loop enables you to declare the loop control variables. Such variables exist in the scope of the loop. The inner for loop in listing 6.1 shows this feature.

Listing 6.1 includes an example of the fixed loop. In this example, the program prompts you to enter an integer in the range of 1 to 50 and calculates the factorial number for that integer. The program uses a fixed loop to get the factorial. If you enter a number outside the range of 1 to 50, the program displays an error message.

Listing 6.1. The source code for the LST06_01.CPP program.

```cpp
// LST06_01.CPP
// Program calculates a factorial using a for loop

#include <iostream.h>
#include <conio.h>

main()
{
    // factorial is declared and also initialized
    double factorial = 1.0;
    int n;

    clrscr();
    cout << "Enter the factorial of [1..30]: ";
    cin >> n;
    if (n > 0 && n <= 30) {
        for (int i = 1; i <= n; i++)
            factorial *= (double) i;
        cout << n << "! = " << factorial << "\n";
    }
    else
        cout << "Sorry! factorial is out of range\n";
    return 0;
}
```

Listing 6.1 uses the following loop to calculate the factorial:

```cpp
for (int i = 1; i <= n; i++)
    factorial *= (double) i;
```

Notice that the loop declares the loop control variable i. The loop uses this variable to update the value stored in the variable factorial. The loop initializes the loop control variable by assigning it a value of 1. The loop continuation test is the expression i <= n. The loop increment clause is i++, which increments the loop control variable by 1. You can write the loop in listing 6.1 in two other ways:

```cpp
for (int i = 1; i <= n; i += 1)
    factorial *= (double) i;
```

or

```
for (int i = 1; i <= n; i = i + 1)
    factorial *= (double) i;
```

The loop increment in listing 6.1 is the best form and the one typically used by C++ programmers.

You can modify the program in listing 6.1 to use a downward-counting `for` loop. Here is how such a loop would look:

```
for (int i = n; i > 0; i--)
    factorial *= (double) i;
```

To use increments other than one, you can rewrite the `for` loop in listing 6.1 as follows:

```
for (int i = 1; i <= n; i += 2)
      factorial *= (double) i * (i + 1);
if ((n/2)*2) != n) factorial /= n+1;
```

This `for` loop iterates about half as many times as the one in listing 6.1. Each iteration multiplies the variable factorial by the expression `i * (i + 1)`. The `if` statement after the loop adjusts the result for odd values of variable `n`.

The program shown in listing 6.2 modifies listing 6.1 so that the `for` loop uses only the loop continuation test. What about the other two components of the `for` loop? The loop control variable, `i`, is declared with the other local variables in the `main()` function. The variable `i` also is initialized with the value of `1`. Consequently, the `for` loop need neither declare nor initialize the loop control variable. As for the loop increment, the post-increment operator is used in the statement that updates the factorial value. This approach absolves the loop itself from incrementing the control variable.

Listing 6.2. The source code for the LST06_02.CPP program.

```
// LST06_02.CPP
// Program calculates a factorial using a for loop

#include <iostream.h>
#include <conio.h>

main()
{
    // factorial is declared and also initialized
    double factorial = 1.0;
    int n, i = 1;

    clrscr();
```

(continues)

Listing 6.2. Continued

```
        cout << "Enter the factorial of [1..30]: ";
        cin >> n;
        if (n > 0 && n <= 30) {
            for (; i <= n;)
                factorial *= (double) i++;
            cout << n << "! = " << factorial << "\n";
        }
        else
            cout << "Sorry! factorial is out of range\n";
        return 0;
    }
```

Arrays

C++ supports arrays that vary in dimensions. The typical number of array dimensions used in most applications decreases as the number of dimensions increases. Most applications utilize single-dimensional arrays. Some programs use two-dimensional arrays, and a few specialized applications employ three-dimensional arrays or higher.

Single-Dimensional Arrays

C++ supports single-dimensional and multi-dimensional arrays. You can declare arrays for the predefined data types as well as for user-defined types.

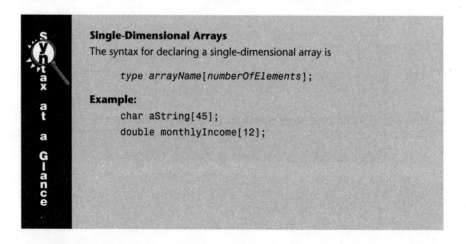

Single-Dimensional Arrays

The syntax for declaring a single-dimensional array is

```
    type arrayName[numberOfElements];
```

Example:
```
    char aString[45];
    double monthlyIncome[12];
```

C++ supports arrays of different dimensions and requires you to observe the following rules:

■ The lower bound of any dimension in a C++ array is set at 0. You cannot override or alter this lower bound.

■ Declaring a C++ array entails specifying the number of members in each dimension. Keep in mind that the upper bound is equal to the number of members, minus one. In the case of array aString, as shown in the preceding example, the range of valid array indices is 0 to 44.

■ Declaring and using an array in an expression requires enclosing the array indices for each dimension in a separate set of square brackets.

The following example illustrates a simple program that uses arrays. Listing 6.3 contains the source code for program LST06_03.CPP. The program declares the array factorial to store the factorials of 0 to 8. The code uses a for loop to calculate the factorials for the elements at index 1 to 8. The program initializes the array element factorial[0] before the first for loop executes. Each loop iteration uses the factorial[i-1], obtained either from a previous loop iteration or from the pre-loop initialization. The program uses a second for loop (this one a downward-counting loop) to display the factorial values in array factorial.

Listing 6.3. The source code for the LST06_03.CPP program.

```
// LST06_03.CPP
// Program calculates a factorial using an array

#include <iostream.h>
#include <conio.h>

const MAX_FACTORIAL = 8;

main()
{
    double factorial[MAX_FACTORIAL + 1];
    int n;

    clrscr();
    // initialize array of factorials
    factorial[0] = 1;
    for (int i = 1; i <= MAX_FACTORIAL; i++)
      factorial[i] = i * factorial[i-1];

    for (i = MAX_FACTORIAL; i >= 0; i--)
      cout << i << "! = " << factorial[i] << "\n";
    return 0;
}
```

Here is the output of the program in listing 6.3:

```
8! = 40320
7! = 5040
6! = 720
5! = 120
4! = 24
3! = 6
2! = 2
1! = 1
0! = 1
```

C++ enables you to declare and initialize an array in one step. For example, the array factorial in Listing 6.3 can be explicitly initialized using the following statements (instead of using a loop):

```
double factorial[MAX_FACTORIAL + 1] = { 1, 1, 2, 6, 24, 120,
                                         720, 5040, 40320 }
```

The number of items contained in the list of initializing values must be equal to or less than the size of the array. If the list size is smaller than the array size, the C++ compiler assigns zeros to the trailing array elements that do not receive initializing values.

Another feature in C++ enables the size of an initializing list to determine the size of the initialized array. The following code fragments show how you can apply this feature to the array factorial:

```
double factorial[] = { 1, 1, 2, 6, 24, 120, 720, 5040, 40320 }
unsigned arraySize = sizeof(factorial) / sizeof(double);
```

The declaration for the variable arraySize stores the actual number of elements of array factorial. The program calculates the number of array elements using the ratio of the total array's size (that is, sizeof(factorial)) to the size of the individual array element (that is, sizeof(double)). You can generalize this method to get the number of elements in any array that is declared and initialized in using a list of initial values.

Matrices

Matrices are two-dimensional arrays that use two indices to access their elements.

Two-Dimensional Arrays

The syntax for declaring a two-dimensional array is

```
type arrayName[numberOfRows][numberOfColumns];
```

Example:

```
char Screen[25][80];
double dailyIncome[12][31];
```

The following simple example demonstrates using matrices. Listing 6.4 shows the source code for program LST06_04.CPP. The program performs the following tasks:

1. Declares the double-typed matrix `mat` with 10 rows and 3 columns.

2. Declares the double-typed array `sumCol` to have three elements.

3. Assigns random numbers to the elements of the matrix. This task uses a pair of nested `for` loops to iterate over the matrix rows and columns. The outer loop also assigns `0` to the various elements of array `sumCol`. The functions `randomize()` and `random()` are declared in the STDLIB.H header file. The function `randomize()` reseeds the random-number generator. The function `random(n)` returns random values in the range of `0` to *n*.

4. Adds the values of each matrix column in the elements of array `sumCol`. This task also uses a pair of nested `for` loops.

5. Displays the sums of columns that are stored in the array `sumCol`.

Listing 6.4. The source code for the LST06_04.CPP program.

```
// LST06_04.CPP
// Program demonstrates using matrices

#include <iostream.h>
#include <conio.h>
#include <stdlib.h>
```

(continues)

Listing 6.4. Continued

```
const MAX_ROWS = 10;
const MAX_COLS =  3;

main()
{
    double mat[MAX_ROWS][MAX_COLS];
    double sumCol[MAX_COLS];
    int row, col;

    clrscr();
    randomize();
    for (row = 0; row < MAX_ROWS; row++)
      for (col = 0; col < MAX_COLS; col++) {
        sumCol[col] = 0;
        mat[row][col] = random(1000) / (random(500) + 1);
      }

    for (row = 0; row < MAX_ROWS; row++)
      for (col = 0; col < MAX_COLS; col++)
        sumCol[col] += mat[row][col];

    for (col = 0; col < MAX_COLS; col++)
      cout << "Sum of column #" << col << " = "
          << sumCol[col] << "\n";
    return 0;
}
```

The following sample output is generated by the program in listing 6.4:

```
Sum of column #0 = 133
Sum of column #1 = 83
Sum of column #2 = 411
```

Because the program uses random numbers, it generates different results for each run.

Multi-Dimensional Array Storage

C++ also enables you to declare and initialize multi-dimensional arrays. The process is very similar to initializing a single-dimensional array. However, you need to know the rule of assigning values to a multi-dimensional array. This rule is based on how C++ stores the array elements. Consider a simple example of a matrix, Mat, with two rows and three columns. The sequence of storing the matrix elements is

```
Mat[0][0] Mat[0][1] Mat[0][2] Mat[1][0] Mat[1][1]  ...
```

Listing 6.5 contains the source code for program LST06_05.CPP. This program resembles that of listing 6.4, except the double-typed matrix mat is assigned fixed values rather than random numbers. The program also uses an initializing list for the array sumCol. The other tasks performed by the program in listing 6.5 resemble tasks 4 and 5 in the list of tasks presented for listing 6.4.

Listing 6.5. The source code for the LST06_05.CPP program.

```
// LST06_05.CPP
// Program demonstrates using matrices

#include <iostream.h>
#include <conio.h>

const MAX_ROWS = 2;
const MAX_COLS = 3;

main()
{
    double mat[MAX_ROWS][MAX_COLS] = { 1, 2 , 30,
                                       40, 500, 600 };
    double sumCol[MAX_COLS] = { 0, 0, 0 };

    clrscr();
    for (int row = 0; row < MAX_ROWS; row++)
      for (int col = 0; col < MAX_COLS; col++)
          sumCol[col] += mat[row][col];

    for (int col = 0; col < MAX_COLS; col++)
      cout << "Sum of column #" << col << " = "
           << sumCol[col] << "\n";
    return 0;
}
```

The program in listing 6.5 generates the following output:

```
Sum of column #0 = 41
Sum of column #1 = 502
Sum of column #2 = 630
```

Using *for* Loops to Create Open Loops

The introduction to the C++ for loop mentions that the three components of the for loop are optional. In fact, C++ enables you to leave these three components empty. The result is an open loop. It is worthwhile to point out that other languages such as Ada and Modula-2 do support formal open loops and mechanisms to exit these loops. C++ enables you to exit from a loop in one of the following two ways:

■ The break statement causes the program execution to resume after the end of the current loop. Use the break statement when you want to exit a for loop and resume with the remainder of the program. Turbo Pascal has no construct that resembles the break statement.

■ The exit() function (declared in the STDLIB.H header file) enables you to exit the program. The exit() function works just like the Turbo Pascal HALT intrinsic. Use the exit() function if you want to stop iterating and also exit the program.

The LST06_06.CPP program, shown in listing 6.6, uses an open loop to repeatedly prompt you for a number. The program displays your input along with its square value. The program then asks whether you want to calculate the square of another number. If you type **Y** or **y**, the program performs another iteration. Otherwise, the program halts. As long as you keep typing **Y** or **y** for the latter prompt, the program keeps running—until the computer breaks down! The code for the LST06_06.CPP program is as follows:

Listing 6.6. The source code for the LST06_06.CPP program.

```
// LST06_06.CPP
// Program demonstrates using the for
// loop to emulate an infinite loop

#include <iostream.h>
#include <stdlib.h>
#include <conio.h>

main()
{
    char ch;
    double x, y;

    clrscr();
    // for loop with empty parts
    for (;;) {
        cout << "\n\nEnter a number: ";
        cin >> x;
        y = x * x;
        cout << "(" << x << ")^2 = " << y << "\n";
        cout << "More calculations? (Y/N) ";
        ch = getche();
        if (ch != 'y' && ch != 'Y')
            break;
    }
    return 0;
}
```

Here is a sample session with the program in listing 6.6:

```
Enter a number: 5
(5)^2 = 25
```

```
More calculations? (Y/N) y

Enter a number: 7
(7)^2 = 49
More calculations? (Y/N) n
```

Skipping Loop Iterations

C++ enables you to skip to the end of a loop and resume the next iteration using the continue statement.

The *continue* Statement
The syntax of the continue statement in a for loop is

```
for (initialization; continuation; update) {
    // sequence #1 of statements
    if (skipCondition)
        continue;
    // sequence #2 of statements

}
```

The continue statement works in a way very similar to that of the other loops that are introduced later in this chapter. The mechanism of skipping the sequence of statements after the continue statement is independent of the type of loop.

Example:
The following example shows how the continue statement works in a for loop:

```
double x, y;
for (int i = -10; i < 11; i++) {
    x = i * i - 9;
    if (x == 0)
        continue;
    y = 1 / x;

    cout << "1/" << x << " = " << y << "\n";
}
```

The for loop in the Syntax-at-a-Glance box shows that the first loop statement calculates the variable x, using the value of the loop control variable i. The if statement determines whether x is 0 (this is true when i = -3 and +3).

If this condition is true, the `if` statement informs the `continue` statement to skip the remaining two statements in the `for` loop.

Exiting Loops

C++ supports the `break` statement to exit a loop. The `break` statement makes the program resume after the end of the current loop.

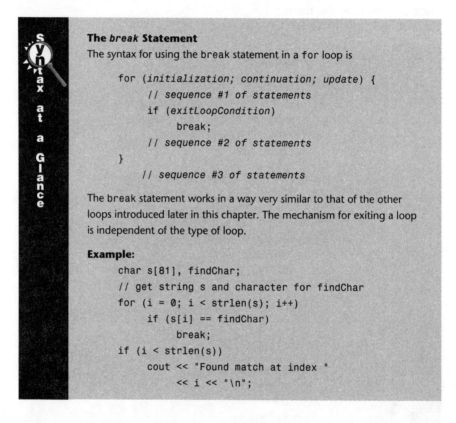

The *break* Statement

The syntax for using the break statement in a for loop is

```
for (initialization; continuation; update) {
    // sequence #1 of statements
    if (exitLoopCondition)
        break;
    // sequence #2 of statements
}
    // sequence #3 of statements
```

The break statement works in a way very similar to that of the other loops introduced later in this chapter. The mechanism for exiting a loop is independent of the type of loop.

Example:

```
char s[81], findChar;
// get string s and character for findChar
for (i = 0; i < strlen(s); i++)
    if (s[i] == findChar)
        break;
if (i < strlen(s))
    cout << "Found match at index "
        << i << "\n";
```

The example code in the Syntax-at-a-Glance box shows how an `if` statement inside a `for` loop can search for a character in a string. While the `for` loop processes each character in the string, the `if` statement inside the `for` loop determines whether the character matches the character being searched (`findChar`). If a match is found, the `break` statement executes and the `for` loop terminates—control then passes to the `if (i < strlen(s))` statement. The function `strlen` returns the length of its string argument and is declared in the STRING.H header file.

The *do-while* Loop

The do-while loop in C++ is a conditional loop that iterates as long as a condition is true. This condition is tested at the end of the loop. Therefore, the do-while loop iterates at least once.

The *do-while* Loop
The syntax of the do-while loop is

```
do {
        sequence of statements
    } while (condition);
```

Example:
The following loop displays the squares of 2 to 10:

```
int i = 2;
do {
        cout << i << "^2 = " << i * i++ << "\n";
    } while (i < 11);
```

The following example uses the do-while loop. Listing 6.7 contains the source code for the program LST06_07.CPP. The program performs the following tasks:

1. Prompts you to enter a string.

2. Converts your input into uppercase.

3. Displays the uppercase string.

4. Asks whether you want to enter another string. If you press the Y key, the program repeats the previous steps.

The program iterates as long as you press the Y key. The loop continuation test checks for your input being the lowercase or uppercase of the letter *Y*.

Listing 6.7. The source code for the LST06_07.CPP program.

```
// LST06_07.CPP
// Program demonstrates the do-while loop

#include <iostream.h>
#include <conio.h>
```

(continues)

Listing 6.7. Continued

```
#include <string.h>

main()
{
    char c, aString[81];

    clrscr();
    do {
        cout << "Enter a string: ";
        cin.getline(aString, 80);
        strupr(aString);
        cout << aString << "\n"
             << "Enter another string? (Y/N) ";
        c = getche(); cout << "\n";
    } while (c == 'Y' ¦¦ c == 'y');
    return 0;
}
```

The function strupr converts the characters of its string argument into upper-case. The function is declared in the STRING.H header file. The following example shows a sample session with the program in listing 6.7:

```
Enter a string: C++ is terrific
C++ IS TERRIFIC

Enter another string? (Y/N) n
Press any key to end the program...
```

The *while* Loop

C++'s while loop is another conditional loop that iterates as long as a condition is true. The while loop may never iterate if the tested condition is initially false.

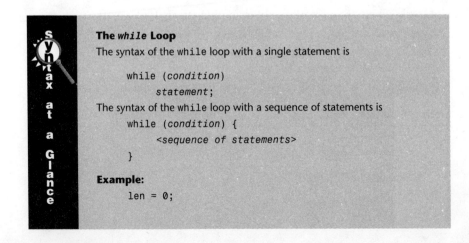

Syntax at a Glance

The *while* Loop
The syntax of the while loop with a single statement is

```
        while (condition)
            statement;
```
The syntax of the while loop with a sequence of statements is
```
        while (condition) {
            <sequence of statements>
        }
```
Example:
```
        len = 0;
```

```
        while (aString[len] != '\0')
             len++;
        i = 0;
        while (i < len)
             if (aString[i] != findChar)
                  i++;
             else
                  break;
```

Consider a program that uses the while loop, such as that shown in listing 6.8. This listing contains the source code for the program LST06_08.CPP. The program prompts you to enter a string and then uses a while loop to count the number of characters as well as the number of space characters in your input. The condition tested for iterating the while loop is the expression aString[i] == '\0'. This expression is true as long as the scanned character in your input string is not the null terminator.

Listing 6.8. The source code for the LST06_08.CPP program.

```
// LST06_08.CPP
// Program demonstrates the while loop

#include <iostream.h>
#include <conio.h>

main()
{
   char aString[81];
   int i = 0, count = 0;

   clrscr();
   cout << "Enter a string: ";
   cin.getline(aString, 80);
   while (aString[i] != '\0') {
     if (aString[i] == ' ')
         count++;
     i++;
   }
   cout << "Your input is " << i - 1
        << " characters long and contains "
        << count << " spaces\n";
   return 0;
}
```

The following is a sample session with the program in listing 6.8:

```
Enter a string: C++ is the best language
Your input is 24 characters long and contains 4 spaces
```

Summary

This chapter covered the C++ loops and topics related to loops. In this chapter, you learned about the following subjects:

- The for loop, which contains three components: the loop initialization, the loop continuation condition, and the increment/decrement of the loop variables.

- Arrays—popular data structures that enable you to store a collection of indexable data items. C++ supports single-dimensional and multi-dimensional arrays. When you declare an array, you specify the number of elements in each dimension, enclosed in a separate set of brackets. C++ fixes the lower index for each dimension at 0. C++ also requires you to use separate sets of brackets for each array dimension when you use that array in an expression.

- Open loops—for loops with empty components. The break statement enables you to exit the current loop and resume program execution at the first statement that comes after the loop. The exit() function (declared in STDLIB.H) enables you to make a critical loop exit by halting the C++ program altogether.

- The continue statement, which enables you to jump to the end of the loop and resume with the next iteration. The advantage of the continue statement is that it does not require any labels to direct program execution.

- The do-while loop, which iterates at least once because its condition check is placed at the end of the loop.

- The while loop, which may not iterate because the condition is checked at the start of the loop. If the while loop's tested condition is initially false, the loop doesn't iterate.

Chapter 7

Enumerated and Structured Data Types

Type Definition in C++

C++ offers the `typedef` keyword, which enables you to define new data type names as aliases of existing types.

The *typedef* Keyword
The syntax of typedef is

```
typedef knownType newType;
```

Example:
```
typedef unsigned word;
typedef unsigned char BOOLEAN;
type unsigned char BYTE;
```

The `typedef` defines a new type from a known type. You can use `typedef` to create aliases that shorten the names of existing data types. You also can use `typedef` to define the name of an array type.

The capability to create user-defined data types is among the features expected of modern programming languages. This chapter looks at the enumerated data types and structures that enable you to better organize your data. In this chapter, you learn about the following topics:

- Type definition using typedef

- Enumerated data types

- Structures

- Unions

Defining the Name of an Array Type

The syntax for defining the name of an array type is

```
typedef baseType arrayTypeName[arraySize];
```

Example:

```
typedef double realArray[10];
typedef double realMatrix[10][30];
main()
{
  realArray x; // declare array
  realMatrix mat; // declare matrix
  for (unsigned row = 0; row < 10; row++) {
    x[row] = 0;
    for (unsigned col = 0; col < 30; col++)
      mat[row][col] = (row != col) ? 1 : 0;
    }
    // other statements to manipulate the arrays
}
```

The typedef statement defines the *arrayTypeName* with a basic type and size of *baseType* and *arraySize*, respectively.

Enumerated Data Types

An *enumerated type* defines a list of unique identifiers and associates values with these identifiers. When you work with enumerated types, always remember one rule: Although the enumerated identifiers must be unique, the values assigned to them need not be.

Declaring an Enumerated Type

The syntax for declaring an enumerated type is

```
enum enumType { <enumeratedList> };
```

The *enumeratedList* is a list of enumerated identifiers.

Example:

```
enum Boolean { false, true };
enum color { black, white, red,
              blue, green, yellow };
```

The following program fragment is another example of declaring an enumerated type:

```
enum diskCapacity { dsk360, dsk720, dsk1_2, dsk1_4, dsk2_8 };
```

C++ associates integer values with the enumerated identifiers. In the preceding type, for example, the compiler assigns 0 to dsk360, 1 to dsk720, and so on.

C++ is very flexible in declaring enumerated types. The language enables you to explicitly assign a value to an enumerated identifier, for example:

```
enum weekDay { Sun = 1, Mon, Tue, Wed, Thu, Fri, Sat };
```

This declaration explicitly assigns 1 to the enumerated identifier Sun. The compiler then assigns the next integer, 2, to the next identifier, Mon, and so on. C++ enables you to explicitly assign a value to each member of the enumerated list. Moreover, these values need not be unique. The following examples demonstrate the flexibility in declaring enumerated types in C++:

```
// explicit value assignment for every list member
enum colors { black = 1, red = 2, blue = 3, green = 5,
              yellow = 7, white = 11 };

// intermittent value assignment
enum colors { black = 1, red, blue, green = 5,
              yellow = 7, white = 11 };

enum choiceType { false, true, dont_care = 0 };
```

In the last example, the compiler associates the identifier false with 0 by default. The compiler also associates the value 0 with dont_care, however, because of the explicit assignment.

C++ enables you to use the following two methods to declare variables that have enumerated types:

■ The declaration of the enumerated type may include the declaration of the variables of that type. The general syntax is

```
enum enumType { <list of enumerated identifiers> }
               <list of variables>;
```

Here is an example:

```
enum weekDay { Sun = 1, Mon, Tue, Wed, Thu, Fri, Sat }
         recycleDay, payDay, movieDay;
```

■ The enumerated type and its variables may be declared separately.

```
enum enumType { <list of enumerated identifiers> };
enumType var1, var2, ..., varN;
```

The program LST07_01.CPP, shown in listing 7.1, uses an enumerated type to model the weekdays. The program prompts you to enter a number that corresponds to a weekday; the program then responds in one of the following ways:

■ If you enter 1 or 7 (to select Sunday or Saturday), the program displays the message Oh! The weekend!

■ If you enter 6 (to select Friday), the program displays the string T.G.I.F.!!

■ If you enter a number between 2 and 5, the program displays the message Work, work, work!

Listing 7.1. The source code for the LST07_01.CPP program.

```
// LST07_01.CPP
// Program demonstrates the use of enumerated types

#include <iostream.h>
#include <conio.h>

// make global enumerated definitions
enum WeekDays { NullDay, Sunday, Monday, Tuesday,
                Wednesday, Thursday, Friday, Saturday };
enum boolean { false, true };

main()
{
    WeekDays day;
    boolean more;
    char akey;
    unsigned j;

    clrscr();
    do {
        do {
          cout << "Enter a day number (Sun=1, Mon=2, etc.): ";
          cin >> j;
        } while (j < 1 || j > 7);
        day = WeekDay(NullDay + j);
```

```
        switch (day) {
            case Sunday:
            case Saturday:
                cout << "Oh! The weekend!";
                break;
            case Friday:
                cout << "T.G.I.F.!!";
                break;
            case Monday:
            case Tuesday:
            case Wednesday:
            case Thursday:
                cout << "Work, work, work!";
        }
        cout << "\nmore? (Y/N) ";
        akey = getche();
        more = (akey == 'Y' || akey == 'y') ? true : false;
        cout << "\n\n";
    } while (more == true);
    return 0;
}
```

The Borland C++ 4 program in listing 7.1 uses the enumerated types WeekDays and Boolean. The following code is a sample session from running that program:

```
Enter a day number (Sun=1, Mon=2, etc.): 2
Work, work, work!
more? (Y/N) y

Enter a day number (Sun=1, Mon=2, etc.): 1
Oh! The weekend!
more? (Y/N) y

Enter a day number (Sun=1, Mon=2, etc.): 6
T.G.I.F.!!
more? (Y/N) n
```

Structures

C++ supports structures that enable you to define a new type that logically groups several fields or members. These members can be predefined types or other structures.

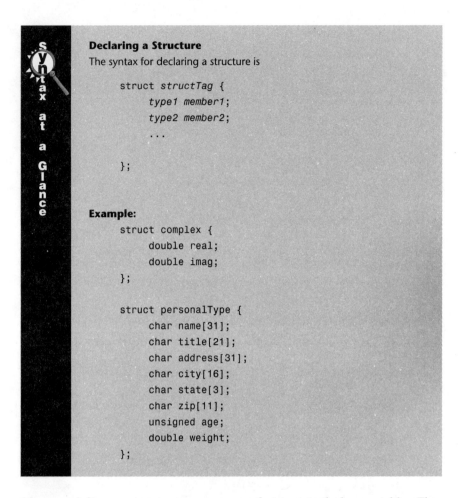

Declaring a Structure

The syntax for declaring a structure is

```
struct structTag {
        type1 member1;
        type2 member2;
        ...

};
```

Example:

```
struct complex {
        double real;
        double imag;
};

struct personalType {
        char name[31];
        char title[21];
        char address[31];
        char city[16];
        char state[3];
        char zip[11];
        unsigned age;
        double weight;
};
```

After you define a struct type, you can use that type to declare variables. The declarations in the following examples use structures declared in the preceding syntax box:

```
complex c1, c2, c3;
personalType me, you, dawgNamedBoo;
```

You also can declare structured variables when you define the structure itself, as shown here:

```
struct complex {
    double real;
    double imag;
} c1, c2, c3;
```

Interestingly, C++ enables you to declare *untagged* structures (and thereby reduce name-space pollution). Using untagged structures involves declaring structure variables without defining a name for their structure. The following structure definition, for example, declares the variables c1, c2, and c3 but omits the name of the structure:

```
struct {
    double real;
    double imag;
} c1, c2, c3;
```

C++ enables you to declare and initialize a structured variable, as shown in the following examples:

```
complex c = { 1.0, -8.3 };
personalType me = { "Namir Shammas", "author",
                    "4814 Mill Park", "Biscaine",
                    "MI", "48104", 38, 190.5 };
```

Use the dot operator to access the members of a structure, as shown in the following examples:

```
c1.real = 12.45;
c1.imag = 34.56;
c2.real = 23.4 / c1.real;
c2.imag = 0.98 * c1.imag;
me.age = 38;
you.weight += 2; // gained 2 pounds!
```

Listing 7.2 contains the source code for the LST07_02.CPP program. This program uses simple structures and an array of structures. The program prompts you to enter four coordinates. The first three coordinates are reference values, and the fourth one is a search coordinate. The program calculates the closest and farthest reference coordinates from the search coordinate.

Listing 7.2. The source code for the LST07_02.CPP program.

```
// LST07_02.CPP
// Program demonstrates using structures

#include <iostream.h>
#include <conio.h>
#include <math.h>

const int MAX_POINTS = 3;

struct TCoord {
    double X;
    double Y;
```

(continues)

Listing 7.2. Continued

```
};

typedef TCoord TPoints[MAX_POINTS];

#define sqr(x) ((x) * (x))

main()
{
  TCoord Coord;
  TPoints Points;
  double MinDistance, MaxDistance, Distance;
  int i, Imax, Imin;

  clrscr();
  for (i = 0; i < MAX_POINTS; i++) {
    cout << "Enter X coordinate for point # " << i << ": ";
    cin >> Points[i].X;
    cout << "Enter Y coordinate for point # " << i << ": ";
    cin >> Points[i].Y; cout << "\n";
  }
  cout << "Enter X coordinate for search point: ";
  cin >> Coord.X;
  cout << "Enter Y coordinate for search point: ";
  cin >> Coord.Y; cout << "\n";
  // initialize the minimum distance variable with
  // a large value
  MinDistance = 1.0E+30;
  // initialize the maximum distance variable with a
  // negative value
  MaxDistance = -1.0;
  for (i = 0; i < MAX_POINTS; i++) {
    Distance = sqrt(sqr(Coord.X - Points[i].X) +
                    sqr(Coord.Y - Points[i].Y));
    // update minimum distance?
    if (Distance < MinDistance) {
      Imin = i;
      MinDistance = Distance;
    }
    // update maximum distance?
    if (Distance > MaxDistance) {
      Imax = i;
      MaxDistance = Distance;
    }
  }
  cout << "Point number " << Imin <<
          " is the closest to the search point\n"
       << "Point number " << Imax <<
          " is the farthest from the search point\n";
  return 0;
}
```

The program accesses the X and Y members of structure TCoord using the expressions Coord.X and Coord.Y. Similarly, the program accesses the X and Y members of array Points using the expressions Points[i].X and Points[i].Y.

The following code results from a sample session with the program in listing 7.2:

```
Enter X coordinate for point # 0: 1
Enter Y coordinate for point # 0: 1

Enter X coordinate for point # 1: 2
Enter Y coordinate for point # 1: 2

Enter X coordinate for point # 2: 3
Enter Y coordinate for point # 2: 3

Enter X coordinate for search point: 5
Enter Y coordinate for search point: 5

Point number 2 is the closest to the search point
Point number 0 is the farthest from the search point
```

Unions

Unions are special structures that store mutually exclusive members. The size of a union is equal to the size of its largest member.

Syntax at a Glance

Union
The syntax for a union is

```
union unionTag {
        type1 member1;
        type2 member2;
        ...
        };
```

Example:
```
union Long {
        unsigned mWord[2];
        long mLong;
};
main()
{
  Long n;
  long m = 0xffffffff;
  n.mLong = m;
  cout << "High word is " << n.mWord[1] << "\n"
          "Low word is " << n.mWord[0] << "\n";
}
```

Unions offer an easy alternative for quick data conversion. Unions were more significant in past decades, when the price of memory was much higher and using unions to consolidate memory was feasible. Today's computers enjoy the abundance of inexpensive memory; saving a few bytes here and there is a petty effort. Accessing union members involves the dot access operators, just as in structures.

Summary

This chapter introduced user-defined data types and covered the following topics:

- The `typedef` statements, which enable you to create alias types of existing types and define array types.

- Enumerated data types, which enable you to declare unique identifiers that represent a collection of logically related constants.

- Structures, which enable you to define a new type that logically groups several fields or members. These members can be predefined types or other structures.

- Unions, which enable you to declare members that share a common memory block. By virtue of their storage scheme, unions enable you to save memory and perform automatic data conversion.

Chapter 8

Pointers

Reference Variables

C++ supports a special type of association between variables, using reference variables. A reference variable becomes an alias for the variable it refers to. Reference variables are used in advanced classes and in the parameters of functions (you read more about this topic in the next chapter).

Pointers are vital tools in C++. They enable you to access and process data quickly and efficiently. The success of C++ as a high-level language lies in how well it supports pointers. In this chapter, you learn about the following topics:

- Reference variables

- Pointers to simple variables

- Pointers to arrays

- Strings

- Pointers to structures

- Far pointers

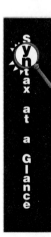

Declaring a Reference Variable

The syntax for declaring a reference variable is

```
type& referenceVar = variableName;
```

Example:
```
int x;
int& y = x;
```

The variable y is a reference (or an alias, if you prefer) to variable x.

You can use reference variables (as aliases) to manipulate the variables they reference. The following example demonstrates such use:

```
int x = 2;
int& y = x;
cout << "x = " << x << " and x (via ref. var.) = "
     << y << "\n";
y *= 2;
```

```
cout << "x = " << x << " and x (via ref. var.) = "
     << y << "\n";
```

The first output statement displays the following output:

```
x = 2 and x (via ref. var.) = 2
```

The statement that doubles the value of y also doubles the value of x. The second output statement inspects the value stored in both variables, x and y:

```
x = 4 and x (via ref. var.) = 4
```

Pointers to Simple Variables

In general terms, a *pointer* is a variable that stores an address of another item, such as a variable, an array, a structure, a class, or a function. C++ requires that you associate a data type (including void) with a declared pointer. The associated data type can be a predefined type or a user-defined structure. This association enables the pointer to properly interpret the data to which it is pointing.

Declaring pointers in C++ is similar to declaring ordinary variables. To declare a pointer, however, you must place an asterisk before the name of the pointer.

Declaring a Pointer
The syntax for declaring a pointer is

```
type *pointerName;
```

Examples:
```
int *intPtr; // intPtr is a pointer to an int
double *realPtr; // realPtr is a pointer
                 //   to a double
char *aString; // aString is a pointer to
               //   a character
```

C++ also enables you to declare nonpointers in the same lines that declare pointers, as shown in this example:

```
int *intPtr, anInt;
double *realPtr, x;
char *aString, aKey;
```

 C++ enables you to place the asterisk character right after the associated type. This syntax, however, does not mean that every other identifier appearing on the same declaration line is automatically a pointer; for example:

```
int* intPtr; // intPtr is a pointer to an int
double* realPtr; // realPtr is a pointer to a double
char* aString; // aString is a pointer to a character
int *intP, j; // intP is a pointer to int, j is an int
double *realPtr, *doublePtr;  // both identifiers are
                              // pointers to a double
```

You need to initialize a pointer before you use it, just as you must initialize ordinary variables. In fact, the need to initialize pointers is more pressing—using uninitialized pointers can lead to unpredictable program behavior or even a system hang!

C++ handles the dynamic allocation and deallocation of memory using the operators new and delete. The operator new returns the address of the dynamically allocated variable. The operator delete removes the dynamically allocated memory accessed by a pointer.

The *new* and *delete* Operators
The syntax for using the new and delete operators in creating dynamic scalar variables is

```
pointer = new type;
delete pointer;
```

Example:
```
int *p;
p = new int;
*p = 2;
cout << "Pointer p accesses the value " << *p
     << "\n";
delete p;
```

Allocating and Deallocating a Dynamic Array

The syntax for allocating and deallocating a dynamic array is

```
arrayPointer = new type[arraySize];
delete [] arrayPointer;
```

The *arrayPointer* is the pointer to a dynamic array.

Example:
```
double *dataPtr;
dataPtr = new double[10];
for (unsigned i = 0; i < 10; i++) {
    dataPtr[i] = (double) i;
    cout << "Element(" << i << ") = "
        << *(dataPtr + i) << "\n"
}
delete [] dataPtr;
```

☞ If the dynamic allocation of operator new fails, it returns a NULL (equivalent to 0) pointer. To avoid potential trouble, therefore, you need to test for a NULL pointer after using the new operator.

The Address-of Operator &

To assign the address of a variable to a compatible pointer, you use the address-of operator &. The syntax of the address-of operator & is

```
pointer = &variable;
```

Example:
```
int x, *p;
p = &x; // p now stores the address of variable x
```

The Reference Operator *

To access the contents of the memory location indicated by a pointer, you use the pointer reference operator *. The syntax of the reference operator * is

```
variable = *pointer;
```

Example:
```
int x = 10, y, *p;
p = &x; // p now stores the address of variable x
y = 2 + *p; // y now stores 12
```

Accessing Arrays with Pointers

A variable is simply a label that tags a memory address. Using a variable in a program means accessing the associated memory location by specifying its name (or tag, if you prefer). In this sense, a variable becomes a name that points to a memory location—in other words, it becomes a kind of pointer.

C++ supports a special use for the names of arrays. The compiler interprets the name of an array as the address of its first element. If x is an array, therefore, the expressions &x[0] and x are equivalent. In the case of a matrix—call it mat—the expressions &mat[0][0] and mat also are equivalent. This aspect of C++ makes it work as a high-level assembly language. When you have the address of a data item, you have its number, so to speak. Knowing the memory address of a variable or an array enables you to manipulate its contents using pointers.

C++ enables you to use a pointer to access the various elements of an array. When you access the element x[i] of array x, the compiled code performs two tasks. First, it gets the base address of the array x (that is, where the first array element is located). Second, the compiled code uses the index i to calculate the offset from the base address of the array. This offset equals i multiplied by the size of the basic array type, as shown here:

```
address of element x[i] = address of x + i * sizeof(basicType)
```

Looking at this equation, assume that you have a pointer ptr that takes the base address of array x:

```
ptr = x; // pointer ptr points to address of x[0]
```

You now can substitute x with ptr in the equation and come up with the following equation:

```
address of element x[i] = ptr + i * sizeof(basicType)
```

C++ simplifies the use of this equation by eliminating the need for you to explicitly state the size of the basic array type. You can write, therefore, the following equation:

```
address of element x[i] = p + i
```

This equation states that the address of element x[i] is the expression (p + i).

The following example demonstrates using pointers to access the elements of an array. Listing 8.1 contains the source code for program LST08_01.CPP. The program calculates factorials and stores them in an array. The program accesses the array elements using a pointer.

Listing 8.1. The source code for program LST08_01.CPP.

```cpp
// LST08_01.CPP
// Program calculates factorials using a pointer to an array

#include <iostream.h>
#include <conio.h>

const MAX_FACTORIAL = 4;

main()
{
    double factorial[MAX_FACTORIAL + 1];
    double *pArr = factorial;

    clrscr();
    // initialize array of factorials using the pointer pArr
    *pArr = 1;
    for (int i = 1; i <= MAX_FACTORIAL; i++)
      *(pArr + i) = i * pArr[i - 1];

    for (i = MAX_FACTORIAL; i >= 0; i--)
      cout << i << "! = " << *(pArr + i) << "\n";
    return 0;
}
```

Notice that the program in listing 8.1 uses the pointer pArr to access the elements of array factorial. The listing uses two forms for accessing an array element with a pointer. These two forms appear in the statement of the first for loop:

```
for (int i = 1; i <= MAX_FACTORIAL; i++)
  *(pArr + i) = i * pArr[i - 1];
```

The first form uses the expression `*(pArr + i)` to access the array element number `i` using the pointer `pArr`. The second form uses the expression `pArr[i - 1]` to access the array element number `i-1` using the pointer `pArr`.

The output of the program in listing 8.1 is as follows:

```
4! = 24
3! = 6
2! = 2
1! = 1
0! = 1
```

Strings

C++ treats strings as arrays of characters. The language uses the null character (ASCII 0) as an end-of-string indicator. This character is also called the *null terminator*. Every string must have a null terminator. Although C++ does not support string operators, it relies mostly on the string manipulation functions declared in the STRING.H header file, developed for C programmers. Table 8.1 lists the string manipulation functions in the STRING.H header file. A detailed examination of these functions is beyond the scope of this book.

Table 8.1. The string manipulation functions in the STRING.H header file.

Function	Description
strcat()	Appends the contents of the source string to the target string.
strchr()	Examines the target string for the first occurrence of the pattern character.
strcmp()	Compares two strings.
strcpy()	Copies one string into another.
strcspn()	Scans a string and returns the length of the leftmost substring that totally lacks any character of a second string.
strdup()	Duplicates the string-typed argument.

(continues)

Table 8.1. Continued	
Function	**Description**
stricmp()	Compares two strings without making a distinction between upper- and lowercase characters.
strlen()	Returns the length of a string.
strlwr()	Converts the uppercase characters of a string to lowercase.
strncat()	Appends, at most, a specified number of characters from the source string to the target string.
strncmp()	Compares a specified number of leading characters in two strings.
strncpy()	Copies a number of characters from the source string to the target string. Character truncation or padding can be performed, if necessary.
strnicmp()	Compares a specified number of leading characters in two strings, while ignoring the differences in the letter case.
strnset()	Overwrites a number of characters in a string with duplicate copies of a single character.
strrchr()	Searches a string for the last occurrence of the pattern character.
strrev()	Reverses the order of the string characters.
strset()	Replaces the contents of a string with the pattern character.
strspn()	Returns the number of characters in the leading part of the string that matches any character in the string pattern.
strstr()	Scans a string for the first occurrence of a substring.
strtod()	Converts a string into a double. String conversion is stopped when an unrecognizable character is scanned.
strtok()	Searches the target string for tokens. A string supplies the set of delimiter characters.
strtol()	Converts a string into a long integer. String conversion is stopped when an unrecognizable character is scanned. String image can be that of decimal, octal, and hexadecimal numbers.
strupr()	Converts the lowercase characters of a string into uppercase.

The C++ string libraries manipulate strings by using the pointers to the pre-defined type char. Listing 8.2 shows a string manipulating program. The program illustrates string input, copying, character conversion, and search.

Listing 8.2. The source code for program LST08_02.CPP.

```cpp
// LST08_02.CPP
// Program accesses a string using a pointer to char

#include <iostream.h>
#include <conio.h>
#include <string.h>

main()
{
    const STR_SIZE = 80;
    char String[STR_SIZE+1], subStr[STR_SIZE+1];
    char cStr[STR_SIZE+1], *p = String;

    clrscr();
    cout << "Enter a string: ";
    cin.getline(String, STR_SIZE);
    cout << "Enter search string: ";
    cin.getline(subStr, STR_SIZE);
    for (int count = 0; *p != '\0'; p++)
      count = (*p == ' ') ? count+1 : count;
    cout << "You entered " << (p - String) << " characters\n";
    cout << "You typed " << count << " spaces\n";
    strcpy(cStr, String);
    strupr(cStr);
    cout << "The uppercase of input string is: "
         << cStr << "\n";
    p = strstr(String, subStr);
    if (p) // same as if (p != NULL) {
      cout << "Substring match at index "
           << (p-String) << "\n";
    else
      cout << "No match for search string\n";
    return 0;
}
```

The program in listing 8.2 uses the `getline()` function to input a string in the standard input stream, `cin`. The program counts both the number of input characters and the number of spaces using a `for` loop. This loop uses the character pointer, `p`, and the variable `count`.

The pointer `p` is initialized by assigning it the address of the input string, which is stored in variable `String`. The loop uses the pointer `p` to access the characters of variable `String`—one character per loop iteration. The loop increments the pointer `p` to access the next character in variable `String`. The iteration stops when `p` points to the null terminator character in variable `String`.

There is one statement in the loop that compares the accessed character of variable String with the space character. If the two items match, the statement increments the value in variable count.

After the loop ends, the program displays the number of input characters. This value is taken as the difference between the addresses of pointers p (which now points to the null terminator in the string of variable String) and String (remember that the name of an array is also the pointer for its base address).

The program also uses the strcpy() function to copy the characters of variable String to the string cStr. Then the program converts the characters of variable cStr to uppercase, using the function strupr().

Finally, the program finds the occurrence of the search string (stored in variable subStr) in the variable String. The code uses the function strstr() to return the pointer to the first matching character stored in variable String. If no match is found, the strstr() function returns NULL. The program uses an if statement to determine whether the function strstr() found a match for the search string. If the program found a match, it displays the index of the main string where the search string appears. The program calculates the value of this index as the difference between the addresses of pointers p and String.

Here is a sample session with the program in listing 8.2:

```
Enter a string: No strings attached!
Enter search string: string
You entered 20 characters
You typed 2 spaces
The uppercase of input string is: NO STRINGS ATTACHED!
Substring match at index 3
```

Pointers to Structures

Assigning the address of a struct variable to a pointer uses the same syntax as that used for simple variables. Accessing the members of the structure, however, requires the -> operator. This operator enables the pointer to the structure to specify a particular structure member.

Accessing a Member of a Structure via a Pointer
The syntax for accessing a member of a structure via a pointer to that structure uses the following expression:

```
structPointer->structMember
```

Example:
```
struct complex {
        double real;
        double imag;
};

complex c = { 1.0, 3.0 };
complex *p;
p = &c; // assign the address of c to pointer p
// access the members of c using p->real
// and p->imag
cout << "c = " << p->real << " +i "
        << p->imag << "\n";
```

For the following example, consider a program that illustrates accessing the members of a structured variable as well as an array of structures. Listing 8.3 shows the source code for the program LST08_03.CPP. The program internally assigns values to an array of structures that model the coordinates of two-dimensional points. The program then calculates and displays the center of the array of points.

Listing 8.3. The source code for the program LST08_03.CPP.

```
// LST08_03.CPP
// Program demonstrates using pointers to structures

#include <iostream.h>
#include <conio.h>

const int MAX_POINTS = 3;

struct TCoord {
    double X;
    double Y;
};

typedef TCoord TPoints[MAX_POINTS];

main()
```

(continues)

Listing 8.3. Continued

```
{
  TCoord Coord = { 0, 0 }, *pCoord = &Coord;
  TPoints Points = { { 1.5, 1.7 }, { 2.2, 2.8 },
                     { 3.2, 3.9 } };
  TPoints *pPoints = &Points;

  clrscr();
  for (int i = 0; i < MAX_POINTS; i++) {
    pCoord->X += (*pPoints+i)->X;
    pCoord->Y += (*pPoints+i)->Y;
  }
  pCoord->X /= MAX_POINTS;
  pCoord->Y /= MAX_POINTS;
  cout << "Center point is at (" << pCoord->X
       << ", " << pCoord->Y << ")\n";
  return 0;
}
```

The program in listing 8.3 declares the structure TCoord and the array of structures TPoints. The program uses the pointers pCoord and pPoints to access
members of structures Coord and Points, respectively. The program utilizes
the expressions pCoord->X and pCoord->Y to access the X and Y members of the
structure TCoord, respectively. Similarly, the program employs the expressions
(*pPoints+i)->X and (*pPoints+i)->Y to access the X and Y members of an
element in array Points.

Far Pointers

The architecture of the Intel 80x86 processors uses 64K segments. The pointers you have used previously in this book store the offset address to the currently used 64K data segment only. What happens when you need to access
an address that lies outside the current data segment? You need to use *far*
pointers. Such pointers store both the segment and offset addresses of a
memory location and, consequently, require more memory. For this reason,
not every C++ pointer is a far pointer.

To declare a far pointer, you place the keyword far between the pointer's
access-type and its name.

Declaring a *far* Pointer
The syntax for declaring a far pointer is

```
type far *farPointer;
```

Example:
```
// access to the view in an MS-DOS program
int far *screenPtr = (int far *) 0xB8000000;
```

To use a far pointer, you need to assign it a far-typed address:

```
farPointer = (type far *) address;
```

For this example, consider a simple DOS program. Listing 8.4 shows the source code for the LST08_04.CPP program. The program writes directly to the color video (assuming that you have a color video adapter) and fills the screen with the letter you type. The DOS program fills the screen with a different letter, using a different color, until you press the letter **Q**. You need to compile this program using the DOS version of the compiler (the file BCC.EXE in the directory \BC4\BIN). Consult the Borland documentation for information on using the DOS compiler. You resort to a DOS program to show far pointers that use absolute addresses because EasyWin programs and Windows applications do not support this feature. Under Windows, you can use far pointers only to store the addresses of variables, structures, and class instances.

Listing 8.4 shows the declaration of the VIDEO_ADDR macro that stores the long-typed address 0xB8000000, the base address of the color video adapter. The program declares the pointer screenPtr in the following way:

```
int far *screenPtr;
```

The program assigns the base address of the adapter to the screenPtr pointer using the following statement:

```
screenPtr = (int far *) VIDEO_ADDR;
```

The following statement then enables the screenPtr pointer to write directly to the screen:

```
*(screenPtr + i) = ch ¦ attr;
```

Listing 8.4. The source code for the LST08_04.CPP program.

```
// LST08_04.cpp
// Program uses a far pointer to write directly
// to a color video screen

#include <iostream.h>
#include <conio.h>

#define VIDEO_ADDR 0xB8000000 // address of a color monitor
#define DISPLAY_ATTR 0x0100

main()
{
  int far *screenPtr;
  long attr = DISPLAY_ATTR;
  const int BYTES = 2000;
  char ch;

  clrscr();
  cout << "Press any key (Q to exit)";
  while ((ch = getche()) != 'Q') {
     clrscr();
     screenPtr = (int far *) VIDEO_ADDR;
     for (int i = 0; i < BYTES; i++)
        *(screenPtr + i) = ch ¦ attr;
     attr += 0x0100;
  }
  return 0;
}
```

Summary

This chapter introduced pointers and covered the following topics:

- Reference variables create aliases for existing variables. Manipulating a reference variable also changes the reference variable.

- Pointers to simple variables offer hooks that enable you to access variables.

- Pointers to arrays are powerful tools that enable your programs to access the various array elements.

■ C++ enables you to use the name of an array as the pointer to its first member; therefore, if arrayVar is an array, the name arrayVar and &arrayVar[0] are equivalent.

■ Strings are arrays of characters that end with the null character. C++ inherits string-manipulating libraries from C. These libraries manipulate strings using pointers to the type char.

■ Pointers to structures use the -> operator to access the various members of a structure.

■ Far pointers empower your application to access data that lies outside the current data segment.

■ To use a far pointer, you need to assign it a far-typed address.

Chapter 9

Functions

Function Syntax

C, the parent language of C++, is more function-oriented than C++. This difference is due to C++'s support of classes, inheritance, and other object-oriented programming features. Nevertheless, functions are essential building blocks in C++. They extend the language in ways tailored to specific applications. In addition, functions support structured programming techniques, because they are highly independent program components. Every C++ program must have the function main(). The programs you have worked with to this point in the book make function main() return an integer value, typically 0. In this respect, the function main() behaves like an ordinary function. These programs also have included many predefined functions. In this chapter, you begin to explore functions you can define to accommodate your C++ applications.

In this chapter, you learn about the following aspects of simple C++ functions:

- Function syntax
- Prototyping functions
- Inline functions
- Using void functions
- Recursive functions
- Exiting functions
- Default arguments
- Overloading functions
- Passing variables by reference
- Passing arrays as function arguments
- Passing strings as function arguments
- Passing structures as function arguments
- Accessing the command-line arguments
- Pointers to functions

Notice the following aspects of C++ functions:

- The return type of the C++ function appears before the function's name.

- If the parameter list is empty, you use empty parentheses. C++ also provides you the option of using the void keyword to explicitly state that the parameter list is void.

- The typed parameter list consists of a list of typed parameters that use the following format:

    ```
    type1 parameter1, type2 parameter2, ...
    ```

    This format shows that the individual parameter is declared just like a variable—you state the type first and then the parameter's identifier. The list of parameters in C++ is comma-delimited. In addition, you *cannot* group a sequence of parameters that have exactly the same data type. You must declare each parameter explicitly.

- The body of a C++ function is enclosed in an open brace ({) and a close brace (}). There is no semicolon after the closing brace.

- C++ supports passing parameters by value and by reference (which you learn about in the following sections).

- C++ supports local constants, data types, and variables. Although these data items can appear in nested block statements, C++ does not support nested functions.

- The return keyword returns the function's value.

Prototyping Functions

C++ requires you to either declare or define a function before using it. Declaring a function, commonly called *prototyping,* lists the function name, the return type, and the number and type of its parameters. Including the name of the parameters is optional, but you must place a semicolon after the close parenthesis. C++ requires that you declare a function if you call the function before you define it, as shown in this simple example:

```
// prototype the function square
double square(double);
```

```
main()
{
  cout << "4.5^2 = " << square(4.5) << "\n";
  return 0;
}

double square(double x)
{ return x * x; }
```

Notice that the declaration of function `square()` does not include the name of its single parameter.

Typically, the declaration of a function is global. You can prototype a function inside its client function. This approach hides the prototype from other functions. Consequently, other functions cannot call the prototype function unless they are declared after the declaration of the prototyped function.

Inline Functions

Using functions incurs the overhead of calling them, passing their arguments, and returning their results. C++ enables you to use *inline functions* that expand, much like a macro, into a set of predefined statements. Inline functions offer faster execution speed (especially where speed is critical) at the cost of expanding the code.

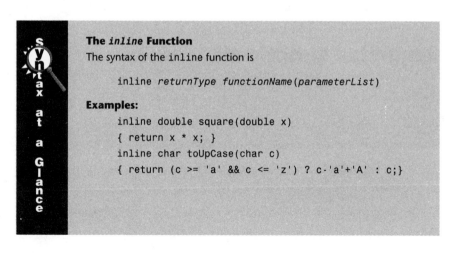

Syntax at a Glance

The *inline* Function
The syntax of the `inline` function is

```
inline returnType functionName(parameterList)
```

Examples:
```
inline double square(double x)
{ return x * x; }
inline char toUpCase(char c)
{ return (c >= 'a' && c <= 'z') ? c-'a'+'A' : c;}
```

The alternative to using `inline` functions is to use the `#define` directive to create macro-based pseudofunctions. Many C++ programmers highly recommend abandoning this method in favor of `inline` functions. The reason for this bias is that `inline` functions offer type checking, which is not available when you use macros created with the `#define` directive.

Void Functions as Procedures

The ANSI C standard recognizes the type `void` as typeless. Consequently, the `void` type enables you to create a form of a procedure that is merely a function that returns a void type. The C++ ANSI committee has adopted the ANSI C standard in supporting and using the `void` type. Before the advent of the `void` type in C, programmers declared the return type to be `int` and discarded the function result by placing the function call in a statement by itself. Some C programmers use the `#define` directive to create `void` as an alias to `int`.

The following simple examples demonstrate `void` functions that clear the screen and move the cursor (these functions require that the ANSI.SYS driver, or compatible, be installed in your CONFIG.SYS file):

```
void clrscr()
{ cout << "\x1b[2J"; }

void gotoxy(int col, int row)
{ cout << "\x1b[" << row << ";" << col << "H"; }

void clreol()
{ cout << "\x1b[K"; }
```

Recursive Functions

C++ supports *recursive* functions—functions that call themselves. You need use no special syntax to indicate that the function is recursive. The following simple example calculates a factorial using recursion. The function `factorial()` returns the factorial of the parameter x by recursively calling itself:

```
double factorial(int x)
// recursive factorial function
{ return (x > 1) ? (double) x * factorial(x - 1) : 1.0; }
```

Exiting Functions

Frequently, you make an early exit from a routine because certain conditions do not enable you to continue executing the statements in that routine. C++

provides the `return` statement to exit from a function. If the function has the `void` type (that is, the function does not return a value), you employ the statement `return`; and include no expression after the `return` keyword. By contrast, if you exit a non-void function, your `return` statement should yield a value that indicates the reason for exiting the function. Here is an example of a non-void recursive function:

```
double factorial(int n)
{
   double product = 1;
   if (n < 2)
      return product;
   for (int i = 2; i <= n; i++)
     product *= (double) i;
   return product;
}
```

Default Arguments

A *default argument* is a new language feature that is quite simple and yet very powerful. C++ enables you to assign default arguments to the parameters of a function. When you omit the argument of a parameter that has a default argument, C++ automatically uses the default argument. Follow these rules when you use default arguments:

■ After you assign a default argument to a parameter, you must do so for all subsequent parameters in the same parameter list. You cannot randomly assign default arguments to parameters. This rule means that you can divide the parameter list into two groups: the leading parameters do not have default arguments; the trailing parameters do have default arguments.

■ In the calling routine, you must supply an argument for each parameter that has no default argument.

■ In the calling routine, you can omit the argument for a parameter that has a default argument.

■ After you omit the argument for a parameter with a default argument, you must omit the arguments for all subsequent parameters.

 When you list parameters that have default arguments, order them according to how likely you are to use their default arguments. Put first in the list those parameters whose default arguments you are most likely to use; at the end of the list, put those parameters with default arguments you are less likely to use.

This simple example that shows the use of default arguments:

```
double power(double base,
             double exponent = 2,
             double errorValue = -1.E+30)
{ return (base > 0) ? exp(exponent * log(base)) : errorValue;}
```

The function power() raises a number to a power. The parameters of the function are base, exponent, and errorValue. The base parameter represents the base number and has no default argument. The exponent parameter represents the power to which the base number is raised. The exponent parameter has the default argument of 2. The parameter errorValue represents the numeric code for an error that results due to using a nonpositive argument for the base number. The default argument for the errorValue parameter is -1.E+30, a large negative number.

The following lines of code are sample calls to function power():

```
z1 = power(x, y, -1.0E+300);
z2 = power(x, y);
z3 = power(x);
```

The first call to function power() passes arguments to all the function's parameters. The second call omits the argument for the last parameter. Consequently, the compiler assigns the default argument of -1.E+30 to the errorValue parameter. The third call uses the default arguments for the second and third parameters. The compiler, therefore, assigns the default arguments of 2 and -1.E+30 to the parameters exponent and errorValue, respectively.

Function Overloading

Function overloading is a language feature in C++ that has no parallel in C, Pascal, or Modula-2. This new feature enables you to declare multiple functions that have the same name but different parameter lists (a parameter list is also called the function *signature*). The function's return type is not part of the function signature, because C++ enables you to discard the return type. Consequently, the compiler cannot distinguish between two functions with the same parameters and different return types, when these return types are omitted.

> **Caution**
>
> Using default arguments with overloaded functions may result in duplicating the signature for some of the functions. The C++ compiler can detect this ambiguity and generate a compile-time error.

This example shows three overloaded `power()` functions:

```
double power(double base, double exponent)
{ return (base > 0) ? exp(exponent * log(base)) : -1.E+30; }

double power(double base, int exponent)
{
  double product = 1;
  if (exponent > 0)
    for (unsigned i = 1; i <= exponent; i++)
       product *= base;
  else
    for (unsigned i = -1; i >= exponent; i--)
       product /= base;
  return product;
}

long power(int base, int exponent)
{
  long product = 1;
  if (base > 0 && exponent > 0)
    for (unsigned i = 1; i <= exponent; i++)
       product *= base;
  else
    product = -0xffffffff;
  return product;
}
```

The first overloaded function raises a `double`-typed base number to a `double`-typed exponent and yields a `double`-typed return. The second overloaded function raises a `double`-typed base number to an `int`-typed exponent and yields a `double`-typed return. The third overloaded function raises an `int`-typed base number to an `int`-typed exponent and yields a `long`-typed return. The overloaded functions are distinctly coded. Each version takes advantage of the parameter types.

The following lines of code are some sample calls to the overloaded function `power()`:

```
double x = 2, y = 3, z;
int b = 2, e = 3;
long a;
z = power(x, y); // call power(double, double)
z = power(x, e); // call power(double, int)
a = power(b, e); // call power(int, int);
```

The first call to function `power()` passes the `double`-typed arguments x and y. Consequently, the compiler resolves this call by using the `power(double, double)` version. The second call to function `power()` passes the `double`-typed variable x and `int`-typed variable e. Therefore, the compiler resolves this call by using the `power(double, int)` version. The last call to function `power()` passes `int`-typed variables b and e. The compiler resolves this call, therefore, by using the `power(int, int)` version.

Passing Arrays as Arguments

When you write a C++ function that passes an array as a parameter, you need to declare that parameter as a pointer to the basic type of the array.

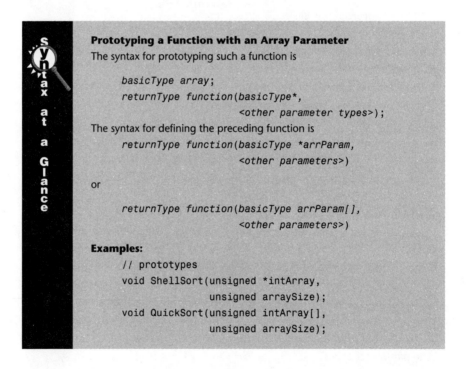

Prototyping a Function with an Array Parameter
The syntax for prototyping such a function is

```
basicType array;
returnType function(basicType*,
                    <other parameter types>);
```
The syntax for defining the preceding function is
```
returnType function(basicType *arrParam,
                    <other parameters>)
```
or
```
returnType function(basicType arrParam[],
                    <other parameters>)
```

Examples:
```
// prototypes
void ShellSort(unsigned *intArray,
                unsigned arraySize);
void QuickSort(unsigned intArray[],
                unsigned arraySize);
```

C++ enables you to declare the array parameter using a pair of empty brackets. C++ programmers use this form less frequently than the explicit pointer form, even though the brackets actually enhance the code readability.

The following code fragment shows an array of integers being passed to a `sort()` function:

```
main()
{
    int intArr[] = { 6, 4, 3, 7, 8, 1, 2, 9, 5, 10 };
    int arrSize = sizeof(intArr) / sizeof(int);
    void sort(int*, int); // prototype the function sort
    sort(intArr, arrSize); // call the function sort
    for (unsigned i = 0; i < arrSize; i++)
        cout << intArr[i] << " ";
    return 0;
}

void sort(int array[], int numElem)
{
    // statements to sort the array
}
```

Using Strings as Arguments

Because C++ treats strings as arrays of characters, the rules for passing arrays as arguments to functions also apply to strings. The following string function converts the characters of its arguments to uppercase:

```
char* uppercase(char* string)
{
    int ascii_shift = 'A' - 'a';
    char* strptr = string;

    // loop to convert each character to uppercase
    while ( *strptr != '\0') {
        if ((*strptr  >= 'a' && *strptr <= 'z'))
            *strptr += ascii_shift;
        strptr++;
    }
    return string;
}
```

The function assigns the address in the parameter string to the local pointer strptr. The function then uses the local pointer to process the characters of the string parameter. Finally, the function returns the pointer string, which still stores the base address of the client string.

Using Structures as Arguments

C++ enables you to pass structures either by value or by reference. This section demonstrates passing structures by value. In the next section, you learn how to pass structures by reference. The structure's type appears in the function prototype and heading in a manner similar to that of predefined types.

The following program code example declares the structure TPoint and uses that structure as parameters of a function:

```
#include <iostream.h>
struct TPoint {
    double x;
    double y;
};

// prototype function
TPoint getMidPoint(TPoint, TPoint);

main()
{
    TPoint pt1 = { 1, 1 };
    TPoint pt2 = { 2, 2 };
    TPoint m = getMidPoint(pt1, pt2);
    cout << "Mid point is (" << m.x << ", " << m.y << ")\n";
    return 0;
}

TPoint getMidPoint(TPoint p1, TPoint p2)
{
    TPoint result;
    result.x = (p1.x + p2.x) / 2;
    result.y = (p1.y + p2.y) / 2;
    return result;
};
```

The call to function `getMidPoint()` passes copies of the structured variables `pt1` and `pt2`. The function `getMidPoint()` works with the copies.

Passing Arguments by Reference

Normally, C++ functions pass arguments by value, submitting *copies* of the original data to the functions. The functions can change the values within them without affecting the original data, which is located outside the scope of the function. C++ enables you to write functions with parameters that pass arguments by reference. Using this kind of parameter, you can change the value of the argument beyond the scope of the function. C++ offers two ways to implement such parameters: pointers and formal reference parameters. The following subsections present functions that pass various kinds of data types by reference.

Passing Simple Variables

You can pass to a function pointers or references to simple variables in order to alter the value of these variables beyond the scope of the function. The following function swaps two integers by passing pointers to the type int:

```
void swap(int* pi, int* pj)
{
  int temp = *pi;
  *pi = *pj;
  *pj = temp;
}
```

The swap() function uses the expressions *pi and *pj to access the integers referenced by the addresses of the int variables i and j in this sample call:

```
int i = 2, j = 90;
cout << "i = " << i << " and j = " << j << "\n";
swap(&i, &j);
cout << "i = " << i << " and j = " << j << "\n";
```

The call to function swap() must pass the addresses of the swapped variables.

The following version of function swap() uses formal references:

```
void swap(int& ri, int& rj)
{
  int temp = ri;
  ri = rj;
  rj = temp;
}
```

The parameters ri and rj are reference parameters; therefore, these parameters become temporary aliases to their arguments within the scope of function swap(). Consequently, any changes made to the parameters ri and rj also affect their arguments beyond the scope of the function swap(). Further, the function uses the parameters without any special access operators. The following example is a sample call to function swap():

```
int i = 2, j = 90;
cout << "i = " << i << " and j = " << j << "\n";
swap(i, j);
cout << "i = " << i << " and j = " << j << "\n";
```

The call to function swap() simply passes the swapped variables, i and j.

Passing Structures by Reference

You can pass structures to functions by using either pointers or formal reference. Many C++ programmers consider either approach as more efficient than passing the structure parameters by value—you save on the overhead of copying the structure.

The following version of the code fragment uses function getMidPoint() and passes its parameters by using pointers and references:

```
#include <iostream.h>
struct TPoint {
```

```
        double x;
        double y;
};

// prototype function
void getMidPoint(TPoint*, TPoint*, TPoint&);

main()
{
    TPoint pt1 = { 1, 1 };
    TPoint pt2 = { 2, 2 };
    TPoint m;
    getMidPoint(&pt1, &pt2, m);
    cout << "Mid point is (" << m.x << ", " << m.y << ")\n";
    return 0;
}

void getMidPoint(TPoint* p1, TPoint* p2, TPoint& mp)
{
    mp.x = (p1->x + p2->x) / 2;
    mp.y = (p1->y + p2->y) / 2;
};
```

The new version of function getMidPoint() returns its result using the third parameter, mp, which is a reference parameter. The first two function parameters are pointers to TPoint structures. In this case, therefore, the reference parameter serves to get information from the called function. In practice, reference parameters that return values are suitable when a function returns multiple results.

Passing Pointers to Dynamic Structures

The binary tree is among the popular dynamic data structures. Such structures empower you to build ordered collections of data without prior knowledge of the number of data items. The basic building block for a binary tree is a node. Each node has a field that is used as a sorting key, optional additional data (called *non-key data*), and two pointers to establish a link with other tree nodes. Dynamic memory allocation enables you to create space for each node and to dynamically set up the links between the various nodes. To learn more about binary tree structure, consult a data structure textbook.

Implementing a binary tree requires (at minimum) functions that insert, search, delete, and traverse the tree. All of these functions access the binary tree through the pointer of its root. Interestingly, operations such as tree insertion and deletion can affect the root itself. In such cases, the address of the root node changes. Consequently, you need to pass a reference to the pointer of the root node, *in addition to* the pointer to the root node. Using a reference to a pointer guarantees that you maintain an updated address of the

tree root. The function in the following sample code inserts unsigned integers
in a binary tree:

```
typedef unsigned int word;
typedef struct node* nodeptr;

struct node {
   word value;
   nodeptr left;
   nodeptr right;
};

void insert(nodeptr& root, word item)
// recursively insert element in binary tree
{
   if (!root)  {
      root = new node;
      root->value = item;
      root->left = NULL;
      root->right = NULL;
   }
   else {
      if (item < root->value)
         insert(root->left,item);
      else
         insert(root->right,item);
   }
}
```

Notice that the first parameter of function insert() is a reference to the tree
node pointer type, nodeptr. This kind of parameter ensures that when you
insert the first item in the tree, you get the updated address of pointer root.
Initial insertion alters the value of this pointer from NULL to the memory
address of the tree root. More complex versions of the binary tree, such as the
AVL tree, the red-black tree, and the splay tree, often rearrange their nodes
and select a new tree root. When you work with these versions of the binary
tree, therefore, passing the reference to the root pointer is even more critical.

Accessing Command-Line Arguments

C++ enables you to access command-line arguments by supplying and using
the following parameters in function main():

```
main(int argc, char* argv[])
```

The argc parameter returns the number of command-line arguments. The
argv parameter is a character pointer that accesses the various command-line
arguments. The value of argc takes into account the name of the program

itself. The expression argv[0] is the pointer to the program's name. The expression argv[1] is a pointer to the first command-line argument, and so on.

The following simple code fragment displays the name of the program and the command-line arguments:

```
#include <iostream.h>

main(int argc, char* argv[])
{
  cout << "Program name is " << argv[0] << "\n";
  for (int i = 1; i < argc; i++)
     cout << "Argument number #" << i << " is "
     << argv[i] << "\n";
  return 0;
}
```

Pointers to Functions

The program compilation process translates the names of variables into memory addresses where data is stored and retrieved. Pointers to addresses can also access these addresses. This translation step holds true for both variables and functions. The compiler translates the name of a function into the address of executable code. C++ extends the strategy of manipulating variables by using pointers to functions.

Declaring a Pointer to a Function

The syntax for declaring a pointer to a function is

```
returnType (*functionPointer)(parameterList);
```

This form tells the compiler that the *functionPointer* is a pointer to a function that has the *returnType* return type and a list of parameters.

Examples:

```
double (*fx)(double x);
void (*sort)(int* intArray, unsigned n);
unsigned (*search)(int searchKey, int* intArray,
                   unsigned n);
```

The first identifier, fx, points to a function that returns a double and has a single double-typed parameter. The second identifier, sort, is a pointer to a function that returns a void type and takes two parameters: a pointer to int and an unsigned. The third identifier, search, is a pointer to a function that returns an unsigned and has three parameters: an int, a pointer to an int, and an unsigned.

Declaring an Array of Function Pointers

C++ enables you to declare an array of function pointers. The syntax is

```
returnType (*functionPointer[arraySize])
              (parameterList);
```

Examples:
```
double (*fx[3])(double x);
void (*sort[MAX_SORT])(int* intArray,
                       unsigned n);
unsigned (*search[MAX_SEARCH])(int searchKey,
                               int* intArray,
                               unsigned n);
```

The first example in the syntax box declares the array of three function pointers, fx. Each member of array fx points to a function that returns the double type and has a single double-typed parameter. The second example declares the array of MAX_SORT function pointers, sort. Each member of the array sort points to a function that has the void return type and takes two parameters: a pointer to an int (which is the pointer to an array of integers) and an unsigned (the number of array members to sort). The third example declares an array of MAX_SEARCH function pointers, search. Each member of the array search points to a function that returns an unsigned value and has three parameters: an int (the search value), a pointer to int (pointer to the searched array of integers), and an unsigned (the number of array members to search).

As with any pointer, you need to initialize a function pointer before using it. This step is simple. You merely assign the bare name of a function to the function pointer.

Initializing a Pointer to a Function

The syntax for initializing a pointer to a function is

```
functionPointer = aFunction;
```

The assigned function must have the same return type and parameter list as the function pointer. Otherwise, the compiler flags an error.

Example:
```
void (*sort)(int* intArray, unsigned n);
sort = qsort;
```

Assigning a Function to an Array of Function Pointers

The syntax for assigning a function to an element in an array of function pointers is

```
functionPointer[index] = aFunction;
```

After you assign a function name to a function pointer, you can use the pointer to invoke its associated function (for this reason, the function pointer must have the same return type and parameter list as the accessed function).

Example:
```
void (*sort[2])(int* intArray, unsigned n);
sort[0] = qsort;
sort[1] = shellSort;
```

Invoking Function Pointers

The syntax of the expression that invokes function pointers is

```
(*functionPointer)(<argument list>);
(*functionPointer[index])(<argument list>);
```

Example:
```
(*sort)(&intArray, n);
(*sort[0])(&intArray, n);
```

The following code fragment includes a pointer to a function:

```
double square(double x)
{ return x * x; }

main()
{
  // declare the function pointer
  double (*sqr)(double);

  sqr = square; // assign function to function pointer
  cout << "5 squared = " << (*sqr)(5.0) << "\n";
  return 0;
}
```

The code assigns the address of function `square()` to the function pointer `sqr`. The code then invokes the function `square()` using the pointer `sqr`.

Summary

This chapter presented simple C++ functions. You learned about the following topics:

■ The general form for defining functions is

```
returnType functionName(parameterList)
{
<declarations of data items>

<function body>
return returnValue;
}
```

■ The `inline` functions enable you to expand their statements in place, like macro-based pseudofunctions. However, unlike these pseudofunctions, `inline` functions perform type checking.

■ The `void` functions are routines that perform a task and return no result.

■ Recursive functions perform an iterative task by calling themselves.

■ Exiting C++ functions takes place using the `return` statement. The `void` functions need not include an expression after the `return` keyword.

■ Default arguments enable you to assign default values to the parameters of a function. When you omit the argument of a parameter that has a default argument, that default argument is automatically used.

■ Function overloading enables you to declare multiple functions that have the same name but different parameter lists (also called the function signature). The function's return type is not part of the function signature, because C++ enables you to discard the result type.

■ Passing arrays as function arguments involves using pointers to the basic types. C++ enables you to declare array parameters using explicit pointer types or using the empty brackets. Such parameters enable you to write general-purpose functions that work with arrays of different sizes. Further, these pointers access the array by using its address, instead of making a copy of the entire array.

■ Passing structures as function arguments enables you to shorten the parameter list by encapsulating various related information in C++ structures.

■ When passing reference parameters, you can use pointers or formal references. The formal references become aliases of their arguments. In the case of passing reference by pointers, such reference can update the address of the argument.

■ Accessing the command-line arguments involves using special parameters in function main(). These parameters get the number of command-line arguments as well as a pointer to each command-line argument.

■ Pointers to functions are valuable tools that enable you to indirectly invoke a function. In fact, using parameters that include pointers to functions enables you to create libraries that can be used with functions not yet written.

Chapter 10

Building Classes

Basics of Object-Oriented Programming

We live in a world of objects. Each object has its characteristics and operations, and some objects are more animated than others. You can categorize objects into classes. For example, my VW Quantum car is an object that belongs to the class of the VW Quantum model. You can relate individual classes in a class hierarchy. The class of VW Quantum model is part of the vehicle class hierarchy. *Object-oriented programming* (OOP) uses the notions of real-world objects to develop applications. The basics of OOP include classes, objects, messages, methods, inheritance, and polymorphism.

Classes and Objects

A *class* defines a category of objects. Each *object* is an instance of a class. An object shares the same attributes and functionality with other objects in the same class. Typically, an object has a unique state, defined by the current values of its attributes. The functionality of a class determines the operations that are possible for the class instances. C++ calls the attributes of a class *data members* and calls the operations of a class *member functions*. Classes encapsulate data members and member functions.

Classes provide C++ with object-oriented programming constructs. This chapter introduces building classes. Chapter 11, "Advanced Object-Oriented Programming," offers more advanced topics related to classes and object-oriented programming. This chapter discusses the following topics:

- Basics of OOP

- Declaring base classes

- Constructors

- Destructors

- Static members

- Friend functions

- Operators and friend operators

Messages and Methods

Object-oriented programming models the interaction with objects as events in which messages are sent to an object or between objects. The object receiving a message responds by invoking the appropriate method (that's the member function in C++). The *message* is *what* is done to an object. The *method* is *how* the object responds to the incoming message. C++ does not explicitly foster the notion of messages and methods as do other OOP languages, such as SmallTalk.

Inheritance

In object-oriented languages, you can derive a class from another class. The derived class (also called the *descendant* class) inherits the data members and member functions of its parent and ancestor classes. The purpose of deriving a class is to refine the parent class by adding new attributes and new operations. The derived class typically declares new data members and new member functions. In addition, the derived class also can override inherited member functions when the operations of these functions are not suitable for the derived class.

Polymorphism

Polymorphism is an OOP feature that enables the instances of different classes to react in a particular way to a message (or *function invocation*, in C++ terms). For example, in a hierarchy of graphical shapes (point, line, square, rectangle, circle, ellipse, and so on), each shape has a Draw() function that is responsible for properly responding to a request to draw that shape.

Declaring Base Classes

C++ empowers you to declare a class that encapsulates data members and member functions. These functions alter the values of the data members.

Syntax at a Glance

Declaring a Base Class

The syntax for declaring a base class is

```
class className
{
    private:
        <private data members>
        <private constructors>
        <private member functions>

    protected:
        <protected data members>
        <protected constructors>
        <protected member functions>

    public:
        <public data members>
        <public constructors>
        <public destructor>
        <public member functions>
};
```

Example:

```
class String
{
    protected:
        char* str;     // pointer to characters
        unsigned len; // current length of
                      // string
        unsigned max; // max length of string

    public:
        String();          // default
                          // constructor
        String(String& s); // copy constructor
        ~String();         // destructor

        void assign(String& s);
        unsigned getLen();
        char* getString();
        String& assign(String& s);
        String& concat(String& s1, String& s2);
};
```

The Sections of a Class

The preceding syntax shows that the declaration involves the keyword `class`. C++ classes offer three levels of visibility for the various members (that is, both data members and member functions):

- *The private section:* only the member functions of the class can access the private members. The class instances are denied access to private members.

- *The protected section:* only the member functions of the class and its descendant classes can access protected members. The class instances are denied access to protected members.

- *The public section:* this section specifies members that are visible to the member functions of the class, class instances, member functions of descendant classes, and their instances.

Rules for Sections

The following rules apply to the various sections:

- The class sections can appear in any order.

- The class sections can appear more than once.

- If no class section is specified, the C++ compiler treats the members as protected.

- In most situations, place data members in the protected section to enable their access by member functions of descendant classes. Avoid placing data members in the public section unless such a declaration significantly simplifies your design.

- Use member functions to set and query the values of data members. The member functions that set the data members assist in performing validation and updating other data members, when necessary.

- The class can have multiple constructors, which usually are located in the public section.

- The class can have only one destructor, which must be declared in the public section.

■ The member functions (as well as the constructors and destructors) that have multiple statements are defined outside the class declaration. The definition can reside in the same file that declares the class. In software libraries, the definition of the member functions typically resides in a separate source file. When you define a member function, you must qualify the function name with the class name. The syntax of such a qualification involves using the class name, followed by two colons (::) and then the name of a function. For example, consider the following class:

```
class String
{
    public:
        String();       // default constructor
        ~String();      // destructor

        void assign(String& s);
        // other member functions
};
```

The following lines of code show the definition of the constructor, destructor, and member function:

```
String::String()
{
    // sequence of statements
}

String::~String()
{
    // sequence of statements
}

String::assign(String& s)
{
    // sequence of statements
}
```

After you declare a class, you can use the class name as a type identifier to declare class instances. The syntax resembles the syntax used for declaring variables.

Example of a Class

Listing 10.1 contains the source code for the LST10_01.CPP program. The listing declares the class Complex to model complex numbers.

Listing 10.1. The source code for the LST10_01.CPP program.

```cpp
// LST10_01.CPP
// simple complex class (version 1)

#include <iostream.h>
#include <conio.h>

class Complex
{
   protected:
     double real;
     double imag;

   public:
     Complex()
       { assign(); }
     void assign(double realVal = 0, double imagVal = 0);
     double getReal()
       { return real; }
     double getImag()
       { return imag; }
     void add(Complex& c1, Complex& c2);
     void print();
};

void Complex::assign(double realVal, double imagVal)
{
  real = realVal;
  imag = imagVal;
}

void Complex::add(Complex& c1, Complex& c2)
{
  real = c1.real + c2.real;
  imag = c2.imag + c2.imag;
}

void Complex::print()
{
  if (real >= 0)
    cout << real << " +i ";
  else
    cout << "(" << real << ") +i ";
  if (imag >= 0)
    cout << imag;
  else
    cout << "(" << imag << ")";
}

main()
{
  Complex c1, c2, c3;

  c1.assign(2, 3);
```

```
    c2.assign(4, -1);
    c3.add(c1, c2);

    clrscr();
    cout << "c1 = ";
    c1.print();
    cout << "\nc2 = ";
    c2.print();
    cout << "\nc1 + c2 = ";
    c3.print();
    cout << "\n\n";

    return 0;
}
```

The class Complex declares two data members, real and imag, that are located in the protected section. These members store the real and imaginary components of a complex number.

The class also declares a constructor (more about constructors in the next section) and a set of member functions. The constructor initializes a class instance by invoking the assign() member function. The class declares the following member functions:

■ The assign() function assigns values to the data members real and imag using the arguments of the parameters realVal and imagVal, respectively. The function has default arguments of 0 for each parameter. The class constructor uses these default arguments to initialize a class instance.

■ The getReal() and getImag() functions return the values of the data members real and imag, respectively. These functions are defined in the class declaration. Each function uses a single statement. The compiler interprets this style of function definition as a request (not an order) to use the function as an inline function.

■ The add() function adds two complex numbers and assigns the result to the targeted class instance.

■ The print() function displays the real and imaginary components of a complex number, using cout. Negative values of either component are enclosed in parentheses.

The following example shows the output of listing 10.1:

```
c1 = 2 +i 3
c2 = 4 +i (-1)
c1 + c2 = 6 +i (-2)
```

Constructors

C++ constructors and destructors work automatically to guarantee the appropriate creation and removal of a class instance.

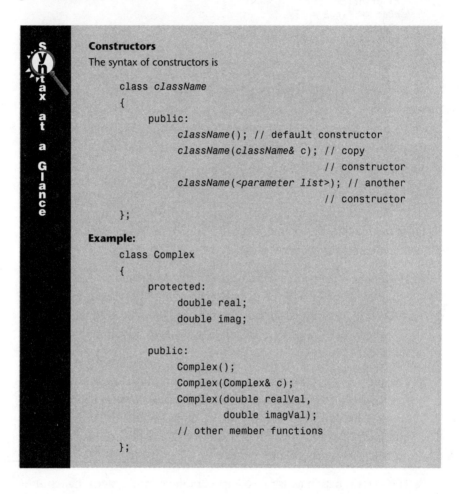

Constructors

The syntax of constructors is

```
class className
{
    public:
        className(); // default constructor
        className(className& c); // copy
                                 // constructor
        className(<parameter list>); // another
                                     // constructor
};
```

Example:

```
class Complex
{
    protected:
        double real;
        double imag;

    public:
        Complex();
        Complex(Complex& c);
        Complex(double realVal,
                double imagVal);
        // other member functions
};
```

Constructor Rules

C++ has the following features and rules regarding constructors:

■ The name of the constructor must be identical to the name of its class.

■ You must not include any return type, not even `void`.

■ A class can have any number of constructors, including none. In the latter case, the compiler automatically creates a constructor for that class.

■ The default constructor is the one that either has no parameters or possesses a parameter list in which all the parameters use default arguments. Two examples of the default constructor are:

```
// class using a parameterless constructor
class Complex1
{
    protected:
        double real;
        double imag;

    public:
        complex1();
        // other members
};

// class using a constructor with default arguments
class Complex2
{
    protected:
        double real;
        double imag;

    public:
        Complex2(double realVal = 0,
                 double imagVal = 0);
        // other members
};
```

- The copy constructor enables you to create a class instance using an existing instance; for example:

```
class Complex
{
    protected:
        double real;
        double imag;

    public:
        Complex(); // default constructor
        Complex(Complex& c); // copy constructor
        Complex(double Real, double Imag);
        // other members
};
```

☞ If you do not declare a copy constructor, the compiler creates one. The compiler uses these constructors in creating copies of class instances. Many C++ programmers strongly recommend that you declare copy constructors, especially for classes that model dynamic data structures. These constructors perform what is called a *deep copy*, which includes the dynamic data. By contrast, the compiler creates *shallow copy* constructors, which copy the data members only.

- The declaration of a class instance (which includes function parameters and local instances) involves a constructor. Which constructor is called? The answer depends on how many constructors you have declared for the class and how you declared the class instance. For example, consider the following instances of the previous version of class `Complex`:

```
Complex c1; // invokes the default constructor
Complex c2(1.1, 1.3); // uses the third constructor
Complex c3(c2); // uses the copy constructor
```

Because instance c1 specifies no arguments, the compiler uses the default constructor. The c2 instance specifies two floating-point arguments. Consequently, the compiler uses the third constructor. The c3 instance has the c2 instance as an argument. The compiler, therefore, uses the copy constructor to create instance c3 from instance c2.

Destructors

C++ classes can contain destructors that automatically remove class instances.

Destructors
The syntax of a destructor is

```
class className
{
    public:
        className(); // default constructor
        // other constructors
        ~className();
        // other member functions
};
```

Example:

```
class String
{
    protected:
        char *str;
        int len;

    public:
        String();
        String(String& s);
        ~String();
        // other member functions
};
```

Destructor Rules

C++ has the following features and rules regarding destructors:

- The name of the destructor must begin with the tilde character (~). The rest of the destructor name must be identical to the name of its class.

- You must not include any return type, not even void.

- A class can have no more than one destructor. If you omit the destructor, the compiler automatically creates one.

- The destructor cannot have any parameters.

- The runtime system automatically invokes a class destructor when the instance of that class is out of scope.

Example of Constructors and Destructors

Listing 10.2 contains the source code for the LST10_02.CPP program. This program typifies the use of constructors and destructors. The program manipulates dynamic arrays that are modeled by the class Array.

Listing 10.2. The source code for the LST10_02.CPP program.

```
// LST10_02.CPP
// Program demonstrates constructors and destructors

#include <iostream.h>
#include <conio.h>

const unsigned MIN_SIZE = 4;

class Array
{
   protected:
     unsigned *dataPtr;
     unsigned size;

   public:
     Array(unsigned Size = MIN_SIZE);
     Array(Array& ar)
       { copy(ar); }
     ~Array()
       { delete [] dataPtr; }
     unsigned getSize() const
       { return size; }
     void store(unsigned x, unsigned index)
       { dataPtr[index] = x; }
     unsigned recall(unsigned index)
       { return dataPtr[index]; }
     Array& copy(Array& ar);

};

Array::Array(unsigned Size)
{
  size = (Size < MIN_SIZE) ? MIN_SIZE : Size;
  dataPtr = new unsigned[size];
}

Array& Array::copy(Array& ar)
{
  delete [] dataPtr; // delete the current array
  // make size of instance equal to size of argument
  size = ar.size;
  // re-create new array
  dataPtr = new unsigned[size];
  // copy elements
  for (unsigned i = 0; i < size; i++)
    dataPtr[i] = ar.dataPtr[i];
  return *this;
```

```
    }

    main()
    {
      Array Ar1;
      Array Ar2(6);

      for (unsigned i = 0; i < Ar1.getSize(); i++)
        Ar1.store(i * i, i);

      for (i = 0; i < Ar2.getSize(); i++)
        Ar2.store(i + 2, i);

      clrscr();
      cout << "Array Ar1 has the following values:\n\n";
      for (i = 0; i < Ar1.getSize(); i++)
        cout << "Ar1[" << i << "] = " << Ar1.recall(i) << "\n";

      cout << "\n\nPress any key to continue..."; getch();

      clrscr();
      cout << "Array Ar2 has the following values:\n\n";
      for (i = 0; i < Ar2.getSize(); i++)
        cout << "Ar2[" << i << "] = " << Ar2.recall(i) << "\n";

      cout << "\n\nPress any key to continue..."; getch();

      Ar1.copy(Ar2);

      clrscr();
      cout << "Expanded array Ar1 (=Array Ar2)"
           << " has the following values:\n\n";
      for (i = 0; i < Ar1.getSize(); i++)
          cout << "Ar1[" << i << "] = " << Ar1.recall(i) << "\n";

      return 0;

    }
```

The class Array declares two data members, two constructors, a destructor, and four member functions. The data member dataPtr is the pointer to the elements of the dynamic array. The data member size stores the number of the array elements. The coding for the class ensures that the array size never goes below a minimum value defined by the global constant MIN_SIZE.

The class defines two constructors. The first constructor, Array(unsigned), has a single parameter that uses a default argument. This argument enables the compiler to use this constructor as the default constructor. The second constructor is the copy constructor, which merely invokes the copy() function to duplicate the elements of one array into the targeted class instance.

The destructor performs the simple, yet necessary, task of removing the dynamically allocated space.

The class Array declares the following member functions:

1. The function getSize() returns the current size of the array.

2. The function store() saves the parameter x at the array index specified by the parameter index. To simplify the code, this example does not include range checking for the index parameter.

3. The function recall() returns the value of the array element at the index specified by the parameter index (again, the code includes no range checking for the index parameter).

4. The copy() function duplicates the targeted class instance using the array specified by the parameter ar. Notice that the copy() function returns a reference to the class Array. In addition, the parameter ar is a reference parameter. Using reference parameters enables you to skip creating a copy of the argument—a step that involves calling the copy constructor of class Array. The copy() function performs the following tasks:

   ■ Deletes the element of the targeted class instance

   ■ Assigns the size member of the argument to the size member of the targeted class instance

   ■ Creates a new dynamic array whose size matches that of the parameter ar

   ■ Uses a for loop to copy the elements of the array ar into the elements of the targeted class instance

   ■ Returns the object *this

☞ When you write a member function that returns the reference to the host class, always return *this. The identifier this points to the targeted class instance, and the expression *this returns the targeted instance itself.

The function main() manipulates the two instances, Ar1 and Ar2, of class Array. The function creates these instances using the following statements:

```
Array Ar1;
```

```
Array Ar2(6);
```

The `main()` function creates instance `Ar1` using the first constructor, acting as the default constructor. By contrast, the function builds the instance `Ar2` by supplying the first constructor with an explicit size. If you place a breakpoint at any statement in the first constructor and run the program, the program execution stops twice at the breakpoint—once for each instance.

The `main()` function assigns values to the instances `Ar1` and `Ar2` and then displays them. The function then uses the `copy()` member function, to copy the size and elements of instance `Ar2` into instance `Ar1`. After copying the arrays, the `main()` function displays the elements of the updated instance of `Ar1`.

The program in listing 10.2 produces the following output:

```
Array Ar1 has the following values:

Ar1[0] = 0
Ar1[1] = 1
Ar1[2] = 4
Ar1[3] = 9


Press any key to continue...


Array Ar2 has the following values:

Ar2[0] = 2
Ar2[1] = 3
Ar2[2] = 4
Ar2[3] = 5
Ar2[4] = 6
Ar2[5] = 7


Press any key to continue...


Expanded array Ar1 (=Array Ar2) has the following values:

Ar1[0] = 2
Ar1[1] = 3
Ar1[2] = 4
Ar1[3] = 5
Ar1[4] = 6
Ar1[5] = 7
```

Static Members

In many applications, you need to use special data members that conceptually belong to the class itself rather than any class instance. Such data members are useful in the following cases:

- Tracking the number of class instances

- Allocating a special memory block for the various class instances

- Using arrays of structures to implement a miniature database commonly used by the various class instances

C++ enables you to use *static* data members for such purposes. When you use static data members, observe the following rules:

- Declare the static data member by placing the static keyword before the member's data type.

- You can access the static members inside the member functions in the same manner you access nonstatic data members.

- You must initialize the static members outside the class declaration, even if these members are protected or private.

- The static data members exist separately from the class instances; you can access them before you create any class instance.

C++ also enables you to declare static member functions to access the static data members. To declare a static member function, place the static keyword before the function's return type. Static member functions *must never* return the expression *this and should not access nonstatic data members.

When you access a public static data member or static member function, you must use the class name as a qualifier.

Example of Static Members
Listing 10.3 shows the source code for the LST10_03.CPP program. This program demonstrates a simple application of static data members. This program is based on the preceding one, but uses static members to keep track of the number of instances of class Array.

Listing 10.3. The source code for the LST10_03.CPP program.

```cpp
// LST10_03.CPP
// Program demonstrates using static data members to count
// the number of class instances

#include <iostream.h>
#include <conio.h>

const unsigned MIN_SIZE = 4;

class Array
{
   protected:
     unsigned *dataPtr;
     unsigned size;
     static unsigned countInstances;

   public:
     Array(unsigned Size = MIN_SIZE);
     Array(Array& ar);
     ~Array();
     unsigned getSize() const
       { return size; }
     static unsigned getCountInstances()
       { return countInstances; }
     void store(unsigned x, unsigned index)
       { dataPtr[index] = x; }
     unsigned recall(unsigned index)
       { return dataPtr[index]; }
     Array& copy(Array& ar);

};

Array::Array(unsigned Size)
{
  size = (Size < MIN_SIZE) ? MIN_SIZE : Size;
  dataPtr = new unsigned[size];
  countInstances++;
}

Array::Array(Array& ar)
{
  copy(ar);
  countInstances++;
}

Array::~Array()
{
```

(continues)

Listing 10.3. Continued

```cpp
    delete [] dataPtr;
    countInstances--;
}

Array& Array::copy(Array& ar)
{
  delete [] dataPtr; // delete the current array
  // make size of instance equal to size of argument
  size = ar.size;
  // re-create new array
  dataPtr = new unsigned[size];
  // copy elements
  for (unsigned i = 0; i < size; i++)
    dataPtr[i] = ar.dataPtr[i];
  return *this;
}

// initialize the static member
unsigned Array::countInstances = 0;

main()
{
  Array Ar1;

  for (unsigned i = 0; i < Ar1.getSize(); i++)
    Ar1.store(i * i, i);

  clrscr();
  cout << "Array Ar1 has the following values:\n\n";
  for (i = 0; i < Ar1.getSize(); i++)
      cout << "Ar1[" << i << "] = " << Ar1.recall(i) << "\n";

  cout << "\nThere are " << Array::getCountInstances()
       << " instance(s) of class Array"
       << "\nPress any key to continue...";
  getch();

  {
    Array Ar2(6);

    clrscr();
    for (i = 0; i < Ar2.getSize(); i++)
      Ar2.store(i + 2, i);

    cout << "Array Ar2 has the following values:\n\n";
    for (i = 0; i < Ar2.getSize(); i++)
      cout << "Ar2[" << i << "] = " << Ar2.recall(i) << "\n";

    cout << "\nThere are " << Array::getCountInstances()
         << " instance(s) of class Array"
         << "\nPress any key to continue...";
    getch();
    // copy elements of array Ar1 to array Ar1
```

```
    Ar1.copy(Ar2);
  }

  clrscr();
  cout << "Expanded array Ar1 (=Array Ar2)"
       << " has the following values:\n\n";
  for (i = 0; i < Ar1.getSize(); i++)
    cout << "Ar1[" << i << "] = " << Ar1.recall(i) << "\n";
  cout << "\nThere are " << Array::getCountInstances()
       << " instance(s) of class Array";

  return 0;

}
```

The new version of class `Array` declares the static `countInstances` member to keep track of the number of class instances. Notice that the program initializes the static data member outside the class declaration using the following statement:

```
unsigned Array::countInstances = 0;
```

In addition, notice that the constructors increment the member `countInstances`. By contrast, the destructor decrements this static data member. These actions enable the class to keep track of the current number of instances as client functions create and destroy them.

The class also declares the static member function `getCountInstances()` to return the value stored in the `countInstances` member. The various member functions access the member `countInstances` just like the other two nonstatic data members.

The `main()` function in the LST10_03.CPP program declares the `Ar2` instance in a nested block. This declaration enables the `Ar2` instance to be created later in the `main()` function and to be removed before the end of the function. When the `main()` function displays the elements of instances `Ar1` or `Ar2`, it also includes the current number of class instances. `main()` displays this information by calling the static function `getCountInstances()`. Notice that this function requires the code to qualify `countInstances` by using the class name, `Array`.

The output of the program in listing 10.3 is as follows:

```
Array Ar1 has the following values:

Ar1[0] = 0
Ar1[1] = 1
Ar1[2] = 4
Ar1[3] = 9

There are 1 instance(s) of class Array
Press any key to continue...

Array Ar2 has the following values:

Ar2[0] = 2
Ar2[1] = 3
Ar2[2] = 4
Ar2[3] = 5
Ar2[4] = 6
Ar2[5] = 7

There are 2 instance(s) of class Array
Press any key to continue...

Expanded array Ar1 (=Array Ar2) has the following values:

Ar1[0] = 2
Ar1[1] = 3
Ar1[2] = 4
Ar1[3] = 5
Ar1[4] = 6
Ar1[5] = 7

There are 1 instance(s) of class Array
```

Friend Functions

C++ enables member functions to access all the data members of a class. In addition, C++ grants the same privileged access to *friend* functions. Friend functions are ordinary functions that have access to all data members of one or more classes. The declaration of friend functions appears in the class and begins with the keyword `friend`. Without the special keyword, friend functions look very much like member functions (except they cannot return a reference to the befriended class, because such result requires returning the self-reference `*this`). When you define friend functions outside the declaration of their befriended class, however, you need not qualify the function names with the name of the class.

Friend Functions

The general form of a friend function is

```
class className
{
    public:
        className();
        // other constructors

        friend returnType
            friendFunction(<parameter list>);
};
```

Example:

```
class String
{
    protected:
        char *str;
        int len;

    public:
        String();
        ~String();
        // other member functions
        friend String& concat(String& s1,
                              String& s2);
        friend String& concat(const char* s1,
                              String& s2);
        friend String& concat(String& s1,
                              const char* s2);
};
main()
{
  String s1, s2, s3;
  s1 = "Hello ";
  s2 = concat(s1, "World!")
  s3 = concat("He said: ", s2);
  cout << s3 << "\n";
  return 0;
}
```

Friend classes can accomplish tasks that are awkward, difficult, or even impossible with member functions.

Example of Friend Functions

Listing 10.4 contains the source code for the LST10_04.CPP program, which offers an example of using friend functions. This program performs very simple manipulation of complex numbers.

Listing 10.4. The source code for the LST10_04.CPP program.

```
// LST10_04.CPP
// Program demonstrates friend functions

#include <iostream.h>
#include <conio.h>

class Complex
{
   protected:
     double real;
     double imag;

   public:
     Complex(double realVal = 0, double imagVal = 0);
     Complex(Complex& c)
       { assign(c); }
     void assign(Complex& c);
     double getReal() const
       { return real; }
     double getImag() const
       { return imag; }
     friend Complex add(Complex& c1, Complex& c2);
};

Complex::Complex(double realVal, double imagVal)
{
  real = realVal;
  imag = imagVal;
}

void Complex::assign(Complex& c)
{
  real = c.real;
  imag = c.imag;
}

Complex add(Complex& c1, Complex& c2)
{
  Complex result(c1);

  result.real += c2.real;
  result.imag += c2.imag;
  return result;
}
```

```
main()
{
  Complex c1(1, 1);
  Complex c2(2, 2);
  Complex c3;

  clrscr();
  c3.assign(add(c1, c2));

  cout << "(" << c1.getReal() << " + i" << c1.getImag() << ")"
       << " + "
       << "(" << c2.getReal() << " + i" << c2.getImag() << ")"
       << " = "
       << "(" << c3.getReal() << " + i" << c3.getImag() << ")"
       << "\n\n";

  return 0;
}
```

The class Complex, which models complex numbers, declares two data members, two constructors, a friend function (the highlight of this example), and a set of member functions. The data members real and imag store the real and imaginary components of a complex number.

The class has two constructors. The first constructor has two parameters (with default arguments) that enable you to build a class instance using the real and imaginary components of a complex number. Because the two parameters have default arguments, the constructor doubles as the default constructor. The second constructor, Complex(Complex&), is the copy constructor that enables you to create class instances by copying the data from existing instances.

The complex class declares three member functions. The function assign() copies a class instance into another class instance. The functions getReal() and getImag() return the value stored in the members real and imag, respectively.

The Complex class declares the friend function add() to add two complex numbers. This short program does not implement complementary friend functions that subtract, multiply, and divide class instances. What is so special about the friend function add()? Why not use an ordinary member function to add a class instance? To find the answer to those questions, consider the following declaration of the alternative add() member function:

```
Complex& add(Complex& c)
```

This declaration states that the function treats the parameter c as a second operand. The alternative member function add() works as follows:

```
Complex c1(3, 4), c2(1.2, 4.5);
c1.add(c2); // adds c2 to c1
```

First, the member function add() works as an increment and not as an addition function. Second, the targeted class instance is always the first operand. Although using the targeted class instance as the first operand is not a problem for operations such as addition and multiplication, it is a problem for subtraction and division. For this reason, the friend function add() works better, by giving you the freedom of choosing how to add the class instances. In addition, you can write overloaded versions of function add() in which the first parameter is not the type Complex. This flexibility gives friend functions an advantage over member functions in providing more flexible ways to write expressions.

The friend function add() returns a class instance. The function creates a local instance of class Complex and returns that instance.

The main() function uses the member function assign() and the friend function add() to perform plain complex operations. In addition, the main() function invokes the functions getReal() and getImag() with the various instances of class Complex to display the components of each instance.

Operators and Friend Operators

The program in listing 10.4 uses a member function and a friend function to implement complex math operations. This approach is typical in C and Pascal, because these languages do not support user-defined operators. By contrast, C++ enables you to declare operators and friend operators. These operators include +, -, *, /, %, ==, !=, <=, <, >=, >, +=, -=, *=, /=, %=, [], (), <<, and >>. (See the various operator tables in chapter 3, "Variables and Operators," to refresh yourself on the use of these operators.) C++ treats operators and friend operators as special member functions and friend functions.

Declaring Operators and Friend Operators
The syntax for declaring operators and friend operators is

```
class className
{
    public:
        // constructors and destructor
        // member functions

        // unary operator
        returnType operator
            operatorSymbol(operand);
        // binary operator
        returnType operator
            operatorSymbol(firstOperand,
                            secondOperand);
        // unary friend operator
        friend returnType
            operator operatorSymbol(operand);
        // binary operator
        friend returnType operator
            operatorSymbol(firstOperand,
                            secondOperand);
};
```

Example:

```
class String
{
    protected:
        char *str;
        int len;

    public:
        String();
        ~String();
        // other member functions
        // assignment operator
        String& operator =(String& s);
        String& operator +=(String& s);
        // concatenation operators
        friend String& operator +(String& s1,
                                   String& s2);
        friend String& operator +(const char* s1,
                                   String& s2);
```

(continues)

```
(continued)

                    friend String& operator +(String& s1,
                                              const char* s2);
                    // relational operators
                    friend int operator >(String& s1,
                                          String& s2);
                    friend int operator =>(String& s1,
                                           String& s2);
                    friend int operator <(String& s1,
                                          String& s2);
                    friend int operator <=(String& s1,
                                           String& s2);
                    friend int operator ==(String& s1,
                                           String& s2);
                    friend int operator !=(String& s1,
                                           String& s2);

      };
```

The client functions use the operators and friend operators just like predefined operators. Therefore, you can create operators to support the operations of classes that model, for example, complex numbers, strings, arrays,
and matrices. These operators enable you to write expressions that are far
more readable than expressions that use named functions.

Example of Operators and Friend Operators

Listing 10.5 contains the source code for the LST10_05.CPP program. This
program is a modification of listing 10.4.

Listing 10.5. The source code for the LST10_05.CPP program.

```
// LST10_05.CPP
// Program demonstrates operators and friend operators

#include <iostream.h>
#include <conio.h>

class Complex
{
  protected:
    double real;
    double imag;

  public:
    Complex(double Real = 0, double Imag = 0)
      { assign(Real, Imag); }
    Complex(Complex& c);
```

```
        void assign(double Real = 0, double Imag = 0);
        double getReal() const
          { return real; }
        double getImag() const
          { return imag; }
        Complex& operator =(Complex& c);
        Complex& operator +=(Complex& c);
        friend Complex operator +(Complex& c1, Complex& c2);
        friend ostream& operator <<(ostream& os, Complex& c);
};

Complex::Complex(Complex& c)
{
  real = c.real;
  imag = c.imag;
}

void Complex::assign(double Real, double Imag)
{
  real = Real;
  imag = Imag;
}

Complex& Complex::operator =(Complex& c)
{
  real = c.real;
  imag = c.imag;
  return *this;
}

Complex& Complex::operator +=(Complex& c)
{
  real += c.real;
  imag += c.imag;
  return *this;
}

Complex operator +(Complex& c1, Complex& c2)
{
  Complex result(c1);

  result.real += c2.real;
  result.imag += c2.imag;
  return result;
}

ostream& operator <<(ostream& os, Complex& c)
{
  os << "(" << c.real
     << " + i" << c.imag << ")";

  return os;
}

main()
{
```

(continues)

Listing 10.5. Continued

```
        Complex c1(1, 1);
        Complex c2(2, 2);
        Complex c3;
        Complex c4(4, 4);

        clrscr();
        c3 = c1 + c2;
        cout << c1 << " + " << c2 << " = " << c3 << "\n\n";
        cout << c3 << " + " << c4 << " = ";
        c3 += c4;
        cout << c3 << "\n\n";
        return 0;
    }
```

The new class `Complex` replaces the `assign(Complex&)` member function with the operator `=`. The class also replaces the friend function `add()` with the friend operator `+`:

```
Complex& operator =(Complex& c);
friend Complex operator +(Complex& c1, Complex& c2);
```

The operator `=` has one parameter, a reference to an instance of class `Complex`, and it returns a reference to the same class. The friend operator `+` has two parameters (both are references to instances of class `Complex`) and yields a complex class type.

The program in listing 10.5 also includes two new operators:

```
complex& operator +=(complex& c);
friend ostream& operator <<(ostream& os, complex& c);
```

 The operator `+=` is a member of class `Complex`. This operator takes one parameter, a reference to an instance of class `Complex`, and yields a reference to the same class. The other new operator is the friend operator `<<`, which illustrates how to write a stream extractor operator for a class. The friend operator has two parameters: a reference to class `ostream` (the output stream class) and a reference to class `Complex`. The operator `<<` returns a reference to class `ostream`. This type of value enables you to chain stream output with other predefined types or other classes (assuming that these classes have a friend operator `<<`). The definition of friend operator `<<` has two statements. The first statement outputs strings and the data members of class `Complex` to the output stream parameter `os`. The friendship status of operator `<<` enables it to access the `real` and `imag` data members of its `Complex`-typed parameter `c`. The second statement in the operator definition returns the first parameter `os`.

The `main()` function declares four instances of class `Complex`: `c1`, `c2`, `c3`, and `c4`. The instances `c1`, `c2`, and `c4` are created with nondefault values assigned to the data members `real` and `imag`. The function tests using the operators =, +, <<, +=. The program illustrates that, by using operators and friend operators, you can write code that is more readable and supports a higher level of abstraction.

The program in listing 10.5 produces the following output:

```
(1 + i1) + (2 + i2) = (3 + i3)

(3 + i3) + (4 + i4) = (7 + i7)
```

☞ The following example also illustrates a special use of the operator [ ]. Listing 10.6 contains the source code for the LST10_06.CPP program. This program uses a dynamic array to calculate, store, and display Fibonacci numbers. These numbers are generated by the following simple sequence of numbers:

```
Fibonacci(0) = 0
Fibonacci(1) = 1
Fibonacci(i) = Fibonacci(i-1) + Fibonacci(i-2)
```

Listing 10.6. The source code for the LST10_06.CPP program.

```cpp
// LST10_06.CPP
// Program demonstrates using the operator []

#include <iostream.h>
#include <conio.h>

const unsigned MIN_SIZE = 10;
const double BAD_VALUE = -1.0e+30;

class Array
{
   protected:
     double *dataPtr;
     unsigned size;
     double badIndex;

   public:
     Array(unsigned Size = MIN_SIZE);
     ~Array()
       { delete [] dataPtr; }
     unsigned getSize() const
       { return size; }
     double& operator [](unsigned index);
};

Array::Array(unsigned Size)
{
  size = (Size < MIN_SIZE) ? MIN_SIZE : Size;
  badIndex = BAD_VALUE;
  dataPtr = new double[size];
}
```

(continues)

Listing 10.6. Continued

```
double& Array::operator [](unsigned index)
{
  if (index < size)
    return *(dataPtr + index);
  else
    return badIndex;
}

main()
{
  Array fibonacci(15);

  clrscr();
  fibonacci[0] = 0;
  fibonacci[1] = 1;
  for (unsigned i = 2; i < fibonacci.getSize(); i++)
    fibonacci[i] = fibonacci[i-1] + fibonacci[i - 2];

  for (i = 0; i < fibonacci.getSize() + 2; i++)
    cout << "Fibonacci(" << i << ") = " << fibonacci[i]
         << "\n";
  return 0;
}
```

The class `Array` models a dynamic array of floating-point numbers with minimal functionality. The class declares three data members: `dataPtr`, `size`, and `badIndex`. The `dataPtr` member is a pointer used to access the dynamic array of doubles. The member `size` stores the number of elements in a class instance. The `badIndex` member provides a value for out-of-range indices.

The highlight of the class `Array` is the operator `[]`. This operator has one parameter that passes the arguments for the array indices. The operator returns a reference to the type `double`. If the value of the parameter `index` is within the valid range, the operator returns a reference to the sought array element. Otherwise, the operator yields the reference to the data member `badIndex`.

The versatility of the operator `[]` comes from the fact that it returns a reference type. Such a return type enables the operator to be used on both sides of an assignment operator. This arrangement is exactly what you see in the first `for` loop located in the `main()` function. Notice that `main()` accesses each element of array `fibonacci` using the operator `[]` as though it were an array of a predefined data type. Using the `[]` operator, therefore, enables you to support a level of abstraction for class-based arrays that is similar to the abstraction offered for arrays of predefined types.

The program in listing 10.6 produces the following output:

```
Fibonacci(0)  = 0
Fibonacci(1)  = 1
Fibonacci(2)  = 1
Fibonacci(3)  = 2
Fibonacci(4)  = 3
Fibonacci(5)  = 5
Fibonacci(6)  = 8
Fibonacci(7)  = 13
Fibonacci(8)  = 21
Fibonacci(9)  = 34
Fibonacci(10) = 55
Fibonacci(11) = 89
Fibonacci(12) = 144
Fibonacci(13) = 233
Fibonacci(14) = 377
Fibonacci(15) = -1e+30
Fibonacci(16) = -1e+30
```

Summary

This chapter introduced C++ classes and discussed the following topics:

- The basics of object-oriented programming. These include classes, objects, messages, methods, inheritance, and polymorphism.

- Declaring base classes to specify the various private, protected, and public members. C++ classes contain data members and member functions. The data members store the state of a class instance, and the member functions query and manipulate that state.

- Constructors and destructors support the automatic creation and removal of class instances. Constructors are special members that must have the same name as the host class. You can declare any number of constructors, or none. In the latter case, the compiler creates a constructor for you. Each constructor enables you to create a class instance in a different way. C++ recognizes two special kinds of constructors: the default constructor and the copy constructor. C++ enables you to declare only one parameterless destructor, in contrast with constructors. The runtime system automatically invokes the constructor and destructor when a class instance comes into and goes out of its scope.

- Static members are special members that conceptually belong to the class itself rather than any particular instance. C++ supports static data members and member functions. Only one copy of a static data member exists, regardless of how many class instances exist. Static data members enable you to store data that is relevant to the class itself, such as the number of instances or an information table commonly used by all the class instances.

- Friend functions are special nonmember functions that can access protected and private data members. These functions enable you to implement operations that are more flexible than those offered by member functions.

- Operators and friend operators enable you to support various operations, such as addition, assignment, and indexing. These operators enable you to offer a level of abstraction for your classes. In addition, they assist in making the expressions that manipulate class instances more readable and more intuitive.

- Friend classes have the privilege of accessing all the data members of a befriended class. Such a relation enables the friend class to quickly and flexibly alter instances of the befriended classes. Such instances typically are parameters that appear in the member functions of the befriended class.

Chapter 11

Advanced Object-Oriented Programming

Declaring a Class Hierarchy

The power of the OOP features of C++ comes from the capability to derive classes from existing classes. A descendant class inherits the members of its ancestor classes (that is, parent class, grandparent class, and so on) and can override some of the inherited functions. Inheritance enables you to reuse code in descendant classes.

In this chapter, you learn about more advanced topics in class and hierarchy designs. This chaper covers the following topics:

- Declaring a class hierarchy

- Virtual member functions

- Abstract classes

- Overloading member functions and operators

- Nested data types

- Friend classes

- Multiple inheritance

Declaring a Derived Class

The syntax for declaring a derived class is

```
class className : [public] parentClass
{
    <friend classes>

    private:
        <private data members>
        <private constructors>
        <private member functions>

    protected:
        <protected data members>
        <protected constructors>
        <protected member functions>
```

(continues)

```
(continued)
        public:
                <public data members>
                <public constructors>
                <public destructor>
                <public member functions>

                <friend functions and/or friend operators>
        };
```

Example:
The following example shows the class TCircle and its descendant, class TCylinder:

```
class TCircle
{
        protected:
                double radius;

        public:
                TCircle(double radiusVal);
                double getRadius() const;
                double setRadius(double radiusVal);
                double calcArea();
};

class TCylinder : public TCircle
{
        protected:
                double height;

        public:
                TCylinder(double radiusVal,
                        double heightVal);
                double getHeight() const;
                double setHeight(double heightVal);
                double calcArea();
};
```

The class lineage is indicated by a colon followed by the optional keyword public and then the name of the parent class. When you include the keyword `public`, you allow the instances of the descendant class to access the public members of the parent and other ancestor classes. By contrast, when you omit the keyword `public`, you deprive the instance of the descendant class from accessing the members of the ancestor classes.

☞ The data hiding feature is justified when a change in context is brought by the descendant class. For example, consider a class that implements a dynamic list of unsigned integers:

```
class intList
{
    protected:
        unsigned* head;
        unsigned listSize;
        // other members

    public:
        intList();  // constructor
        ~intList(); // destructor
        int insert(unsigned n);
        int search(unsigned n);
        int remove(unsigned n);
        void clearList();
        // other member functions
};
```

Now you can use the preceding class to implement a class that models a list-based stack of unsigned integers:

```
class intStack : intList
{
    public:
        intStack(); // constructor
        ~intStack(); // destructor
        void push(unsigned n);
        int pop(unsigned& n);
        void clearStack();
};
```

The class `intStack` is a descendant of class `intList`. However, you do not want the instances of class `intStack` to access the public member functions `insert()`, `search()`, and `remove()` because those member functions support operations for lists, not stacks. By omitting the public class derivation, you force the instances of class `intStack` to use the member functions `push()`, `pop()`, and `clearStack()`. The preceding example shows how the descendant class has changed context but has continued to make use of the operations supported by the parent class.

A descendant class inherits the data members of its ancestor class or classes. C++ has no mechanisms for removing unwanted inherited data members— basically, you are stuck with them. By contrast, C++ enables you to override inherited member functions. You read more about this topic later in this chapter. The descendant class declares new data members, new member functions, and overriding member functions. Again, you can place these members in the private, protected, or public sections as you see fit in your class design.

Example for Deriving Classes

Consider an example that declares a small class hierarchy. Listing 11.1 shows the source code for the LST11_01.CPP program. This program declares classes that contain a hierarchy of simple geometric shapes: a circle, a sphere, a cylinder, and a hollow cylinder.

Listing 11.1. The source code for the LST11_01.CPP program.

```
// LST11_01.CPP
// Program demonstrates a small hierarchy of classes

#include <iostream.h>
#include <conio.h>
#include <math.h>

const double pi = 4 * atan(1);

inline double sqr(double x)
{ return x * x; }

class TCircle
{
  protected:
    double radius;

  public:
    TCircle(double radiusVal = 0) : radius(radiusVal) {}
    void setRadius(double radiusVal)
      { radius = radiusVal; }
    double getRadius() const
      { return radius; }
    double area() const
      { return pi * sqr(radius); }
    void showData();
};

class TCylinder : public TCircle
{
  protected:
    double height;

  public:
    TCylinder(double heightVal = 0, double radiusVal = 0)
      : height(heightVal), TCircle(radiusVal) {}
```

```
          void setHeight(double heightVal)
            { height = heightVal; }
          double getHeight() const
            { return height; }
          double area() const
            { return 2 * TCircle::area() +
                    2 * pi * radius * height; }
          void showData();
    };

    void TCircle::showData()
    {
       cout << "Circle radius      = " << getRadius() << "\n"
            << "Circle area        = " << area() << "\n\n";
    }

    void TCylinder::showData()
    {
       cout << "Cylinder radius    = " << getRadius() << "\n"
            << "Cylinder height    = " << getHeight() << "\n"
            << "Cylinder area      = " << area() << "\n\n";
    }

    main()
    {
       TCircle Circle(1);
       TCylinder Cylinder(10, 1);

       clrscr();
       Circle.showData();
       Cylinder.showData();
       return 0;
    }
```

This listing declares the classes TCircle and TCylinder. The class TCircle models a circle, whereas class TCylinder models a cylinder.

The TCircle class declares a single data member, radius, to store the radius of the circle. The class also declares a constructor and a set of member functions. The constructor assigns a value to the data member radius when you declare a class instance. Notice that the constructor uses a new syntax to initialize the member radius. The functions setRadius() and getRadius() set and query the value in member radius, respectively. The function area() returns the area of the circle. The function showData() displays the radius and area of a class instance.

The class TCylinder, a descendant of TCircle, declares a single data member, height, to store the height of the cylinder. The class inherits the member radius needed to store the radius of the cylinder. The TCylinder class declares a constructor and a set of member functions. The constructor assigns values to the radius and height members when creating a class instance. Notice the use of a new syntax to initialize the members—the member height is initialized, and the member radius is initialized by invoking the constructor of class TCircle with the argument radiusVal. The functions setHeight() and getHeight() set and query the value in member height, respectively. The class uses the inherited function setRadius() and getRadius() to manipulate the inherited member radius. The function area(), which overrides the inherited function TCircle::area(), returns the surface area of the cylinder. Notice that this function explicitly invokes the inherited function TCircle::area(). The function showData() displays the radius, height, and area of a class instance.

The main() function performs the following tasks:

1. Declares the instance Circle, of class TCircle, and assigns 1 to the circle's radius.

2. Declares the instance Cylinder, of class TCylinder, and assigns 10 to the circle's height and 1 to the circle's radius.

3. Invokes the showData() routine for each class instance.

Here is the output for the program in listing 11.1:

```
Circle radius       = 1
Circle area         = 3.141593

Cylinder radius     = 1
Cylinder height     = 10
Cylinder area       = 69.115038
```

Virtual Functions

Polymorphic behavior is an important object-oriented programming feature. This feature empowers the instances of different classes to respond to the same function in ways that are appropriate to each class. Consider the following simple classes and the main() function:

```
#include <iostream.h>
class TA
{
    public:
        double A(double x)
            { return x * x; }
        double B(double x)
            { return A(x) / 2; }
};
```

```
class TB : public TA
{
    public:
        double A(double x)
            { return x * x * x; }
};

main()
{
    TB aB;
    cout << aB.B(3) << "\n";
    return 0;
}
```

Class TA contains functions A() and B(), where function B() calls function A(). Class TB, a descendant of class TA, inherits function B() but overrides function A(). The intent here is to have the inherited function TA::B() call function TB::A(), to support polymorphic behavior. What is the program output? The answer is 4.5 and *not* 13.5! Why? The answer lies in the fact that the compiler resolves the expression aB.B(3) by using the inherited function TA::B(), which in turn calls function TA::A(). Function TB:A() is left out, therefore, and the program fails to support polymorphic behavior.

C++ supports polymorphic behavior by offering *virtual* functions. You declare these functions, which are bound at runtime, by placing the keyword virtual before the function's return type. After you declare a virtual function, you can override it only with virtual functions in descendant classes. These over-riding functions *must* have the same parameter list. Virtual functions can override nonvirtual functions in ancestor classes.

Declaring Virtual Functions
The syntax for declaring virtual functions is

```
class className1
{
    // member functions
    virtual returnType
            functionName(<parameter list>);
};

class className2 : public className1
{
    // member functions
    virtual returnType
```

(continues)

(continued)

```
                    functionName(<parameter list>);
    };
```

Example:
The following example shows how virtual functions can successfully
implement polymorphic behavior in classes TA and TB.

```
#include <iostream.h>
class TA
{
    public:
        virtual double A(double x)
            { return x * x; }
        double B(double x)
            { return A(x) / 2; }
};

class TB : public TA
{
    public:
        virtual double A(double x)
            { return x * x * x; }
};

main()
{
    TB aB;
    cout << aB.B(3) << "\n";
    return 0;
}
```

This example displays 13.5, the correct result, because the call to the
inherited function TA::B() is resolved at runtime by calling TB::A().

 When do you use virtual functions? When you have a callable function that
implements a behavior specific to a class, you declare that function to be a
virtual function. Declaring such a function as virtual ensures that it provides
the correct response that is relevant to the associated class.

Example of Using Virtual Functions

Consider the following example of using virtual functions. Listing 11.2 shows the source code for the program LST11_02.CPP. The program expands the class hierarchy found in listing 11.1. The new version has three classes, TCircle, TCylinder, and THollowCylinder. The THollowCylinder class models a hollow cylinder and is a descendant of class TCylinder. The program calculates and displays the area of the circle, the base area, and the volume of the two cylinder types.

Listing 11.2. The source code for the LST11_02.CPP program.

```cpp
// LST11_02.CPP
// Program demonstrates virtual functions

#include <iostream.h>
#include <conio.h>
#include <math.h>

const double pi = 4 * atan(1);

inline double sqr(double x)
{ return x * x; }

class TCircle
{
  protected:
    double radius;

  public:
    TCircle(double radiusVal = 0) : radius(radiusVal) {}
    void setRadius(double radiusVal)
      { radius = radiusVal; }
    double getRadius() const
      { return radius; }
    virtual double area() const
      { return pi * sqr(radius); }
    void showData();
};

class TCylinder : public TCircle
{
  protected:
    double height;

  public:
    TCylinder(double heightVal = 0, double radiusVal = 0)
      : height(heightVal), TCircle(radiusVal) {}
    void setHeight(double heightVal)
      { height = heightVal; }
    double getHeight() const
      { return height; }
```

(continues)

Listing 11.2. Continued

```
          double volume()
            { return height * area(); }
          void showData();
    };

    class THollowCylinder : public TCylinder
    {
      protected:
        double innerRadius;

      public:
        THollowCylinder(double heightVal = 0, double Rin = 0,
                        double Rout = 0) : innerRadius(Rin),
          TCylinder(heightVal, Rout) {}
        void setInnerRadius(double Rin)
          { innerRadius = Rin; }
        double getInnerRadius() const
          { return innerRadius; }
        virtual double area() const
          { return pi * (sqr(radius) - sqr(innerRadius)); }
        void showData();
    };

    void TCircle::showData()
    {
       cout << "Circle radius        = " << getRadius() << "\n"
            << "Circle area          = " << area() << "\n\n";
    }

    void TCylinder::showData()
    {
       cout << "Cylinder radius      = " << getRadius() << "\n"
            << "Cylinder height      = " << getHeight() << "\n"
            << "Cylinder base area   = " << area() << "\n"
            << "Cylinder volume      = " << volume()  << "\n\n";
    }

    void THollowCylinder::showData()
    {
       cout << "Hollow radius        = " << getRadius() << "\n"
            << "Hollow inner radius  = " << getInnerRadius()
                                         << "\n"
            << "Hollow height        = " << getHeight() << "\n"
            << "Cylinder base area   = " << area() << "\n"
            << "Hollow volume        = " << volume() << "\n\n";
    }

    main()
    {
       TCircle Circle(1);
       TCylinder Cylinder(10, 1);
       THollowCylinder Hollow(10, 0.5, 1);

       clrscr();
```

```
        Circle.showData();
        Cylinder.showData();
        Hollow.showData();
        return 0;
    }
```

The highlight of listing 11.2 is the virtual function area() and the function volume(). The volume of the full cylinder is the product of the height and the base area (which is equal to the area of the circular base). The volume of the hollow cylinder is the product of the height and the base area (which is equal to the net area of the circular base).

The class TCircle declares the virtual function area(). Class TCylinder simply inherits the virtual function, because the values returned by TCircle::area() are adequate for class TCylinder. By contrast, class THollowCylinder declares its own virtual function area() to calculate the base area differently.

Class TCylinder declares the function volume() to calculate the volume of a cylinder. This function uses the inherited virtual function TCircle::area(). Interestingly, class THollowCylinder inherits function TCylinder::volume(). This inherited function performs the correct calculation by calling the virtual function THollowCylinder::area().

Here is the output of the program in listing 11.2:

```
    Circle radius       = 1
    Circle area         = 3.141593

    Cylinder radius     = 1
    Cylinder height     = 10
    Cylinder base area  = 3.141593
    Cylinder volume     = 31.415927

    Hollow radius       = 1
    Hollow inner radius = 0.5
    Hollow height       = 10
    Cylinder base area  = 2.356194
    Hollow volume       = 23.561945
```

☛ C++ programmers highly recommend that you declare the destructor as virtual. This ensures polymorphic behavior in destroying class instances.

Abstract Classes

C++ expands the notion of refining classes by derivation through *abstract* classes. Such classes include the base class of a hierarchy and possibly the first few descendants. The class hierarchy designer can use virtual functions and a special syntax in the abstract classes to influence the evolution of the class hierarchy. The influence over descendant classes occurs through the virtual functions. Remember that when you override an inherited virtual function, you must use the same parameter list.

Abstract Classes

The syntax of an abstract class is

```
class abstractClass
{
    <private members>

    protected:
        // protected data members
        virtual returnType
            function1(<parameter list 1>) = 0;
        virtual returnType
            function2(<parameter list 2>) = 0;
        // other member functions

    public:
        // public data members
        virtual returnType
            function3(<parameter list 3>) = 0;
        virtual returnType
            function4(<parameter list 4>) = 0;
        // other member functions
};
```

Example:

The following class declaration models an abstract array that stores floating-point numbers. The functions store(), recall(), swap(), and reverse() are declared as abstract functions. The other member functions have implementations (not included in the book) that use the store(), recall(), and swap() functions to sort and search for array elements.

```
class AbstractArray
{
    protected:
        unsigned workSize;
```

```
                  unsigned maxSize;

          public:
                  virtual boolean store(double x,
                                        unsigned index) = 0;
                  virtual boolean recall(double& x,
                                         unsigned index) = 0;
                  virtual void swap(index i,
                                    index j) = 0;
                  virtual void reverse() = 0;
                  void quickSort();
                  unsigned linearSearch(double key,
                                        unsigned start);
                  unsigned binarySearch(double key);
          };
```

To give you a better feel for using abstract classes, examine the following class declarations. These declarations are based on the class AbstractArray that appears in the previous syntax box:

```
class memArray : public AbstractArray
{
    protected:
        double* dataPtr; // pointer to dynamic array

    public:
        memArray(unsigned arraySize);
        ~memArray();
        virtual boolean store(double x, unsigned index);
        virtual boolean recall(double& x, unsigned index);
        virtual void swap(index i, index j);
        virtual void reverse();
};

class VmArray : public AbstractArray
{
    protected:
        fstream f; // C++ file stream

    public:
        VmArray(const char* filename, unsigned arraySize);
        ~VmArray();
        virtual boolean store(double x, unsigned index);
        virtual boolean recall(double& x, unsigned index);
        virtual void swap(index i, index j);
        virtual void reverse();
};
```

The class `memArray` implements a heap-based dynamic array, accessed using the pointer `dataPtr`. The class inherits the `quickSort()`, `linearSearch()`, and `binarySearch()` functions. By contrast, the class declares its own version of the virtual functions `store()`, `recall()`, `swap()`, and `reverse()`. These functions use the `dataPtr` member to access the elements of the dynamic array in the heap.

The class `VmArray` implements a disk-based virtual dynamic array. This array uses the stream `f` to access the individual array elements in a data file. This class also inherits the `quickSort()`, `linearSearch()`, and `binarySearch()` functions. Like class `memArray`, this class declares its own version of the virtual functions. These functions use the stream `f` to access the elements of the dynamic array.

Overloading Member Functions and Operators

C++ enables you to overload member functions, operators, friend functions, and friend operators. The rules for overloading these functions and operators are the same, within a class, as those for overloading ordinary functions.

Example of Overloaded Functions

Listing 11.3 shows a simple example of overloading functions and operators, applied to the class `Complex`. The class overloads the function `assign()`, the operator `=`, and the friend operator `+`. Overloading these functions and operators enables you to write abstract expressions and statements. The overloaded assignment statements enable you to assign the individual components of a complex number, or use an existing class instance. The overloaded `=` operator enables you to assign a class instance to another, or assign the real number to a class instance. The overloaded friend operator (`+`) enables you to add two class instances, or add a real number to a class instance. The latter case requires two versions of the operator `+` to ensure that you cover having either added entity as the first or second operand.

Listing 11.3. The source code for the LST11_03.CPP program.

```
// LST11_03.CPP
// Program that illustrates overloading functions
// and operators

#include <iostream.h>
```

```
#include <conio.h>

class Complex
{
   protected:
     double real;
     double imag;

   public:
     Complex()
       { assign(); }
     void assign(double realVal = 0, double imagVal = 0);
     void assign(Complex& c)
       { assign(c.real, c.imag); }
     double getReal()
       { return real; }
     double getImag()
       { return imag; }
     void print();
     Complex& operator =(double realVal)
       { assign(realVal, 0); return *this; }
     Complex& operator =(Complex& c)
       { assign(c); return *this; }
     friend Complex operator+(Complex& c1, Complex& c2);
     friend Complex operator+(Complex& c, double x);
     friend Complex operator+(double x, Complex& c);
};

void Complex::assign(double realVal, double imagVal)
{
  real = realVal;
  imag = imagVal;
}

void Complex::print()
{
  if (real >= 0)
    cout << real << " +i ";
  else
    cout << "(" << real << ") +i ";
  if (imag >= 0)
    cout << imag;
  else
    cout << "(" << imag << ")";
}

Complex operator+(Complex& c1, Complex& c2)
{
  Complex cc(c1);
  cc.real += c2.real;
  cc.imag += c2.imag;
  return cc;
}

Complex operator+(Complex& c, double x)
```

(continues)

Listing 11.3. Continued

```
  {
    Complex cc(c);
    cc.real += x;
    return cc;
  }

  Complex operator+(double x, Complex& c)
  {
    Complex cc(c);
    cc.real += x;
    return cc;
  }

  main()
  {
    Complex c1, c2, c3;

    c1.assign(2, 3);
    c2.assign(4, -1);
    c3 = 2.0 + c1 + c2 + 4.0;

    clrscr();
    cout << "c1 = ";
    c1.print();
    cout << "\nc2 = ";
    c2.print();
    cout << "\n2 + c1 + c2 + 4 = ";
    c3.print();
    cout << "\n\n";
    return 0;
  }
```

The following output is produced by the program in listing 11.3:

```
c1 = 2 +i 3
c2 = 4 +i (-1)
2 + c1 + c2 + 4 = 12 +i 2
```

Rules for Virtual Functions

The rule for declaring a virtual function is "once virtual, always virtual." In other words, after you declare a function to be virtual in a class, any subclass that overrides the virtual function must do so using another virtual function (that has the same parameter list). The virtual declaration is mandatory for the descendant classes. At first, this rule seems to lock you in. This limitation is certainly true for object-oriented programming languages that support virtual functions but not overloaded functions. In the case of C++, the workaround is interesting. You can declare nonvirtual and overloaded functions that have the same name as the virtual function but bear a different parameter list. Moreover, you cannot inherit nonvirtual member functions that share the same name with a virtual function. The following simple example illustrates this point:

```cpp
#include <iostream.h>
class A
{
  public:
    A() {}
    virtual void foo(char c)
      { cout << "virtual A::foo() returns " << c << '\n'; }
};

class B : public A
{
  public:
    B() {}
    void foo(const char* s)
      { cout << "B::foo() returns " << s << '\n'; }
    void foo(int i)
      { cout << "B::foo() returns " << i << '\n'; }
    virtual void foo(char c)
      { cout << "virtual B::foo() returns " << c << '\n'; }
};

class C : public B
{
  public:
    C() {}
    void foo(const char* s)
      { cout << "C::foo() returns " << s << '\n'; }
    void foo(double x)
      { cout << "C::foo() returns " << x << '\n'; }
    virtual void foo(char c)
      { cout << "virtual C::foo() returns " << c << '\n'; }
};

main()
{
  int n = 100;
  A Aobj;
  B Bobj;
  C Cobj;

  Aobj.foo('A');
  Bobj.foo('B');
  Bobj.foo(10);
  Bobj.foo("Bobj");
  Cobj.foo('C');
  // if you uncomment the next statement, program does
  // not compile
  // Cobj.foo(n);
  Cobj.foo(144.123);
  Cobj.foo("Cobj");

  return 0;
}
```

This code declares three classes, A, B, and C, to form a linear hierarchy of classes. Class A declares function foo(char) as virtual. Class B also declares its own version of the virtual function foo(char). In addition, class B declares the nonvirtual overloaded functions foo(const char* s) and foo(int). Class C, the descendant of class B, declares the virtual function foo(char) and the nonvirtual and overloaded functions foo(const char*) and foo(double). Notice that class C *must* declare the foo(const char*) function if it needs the function, because it cannot inherit the member function B::foo(const char*). C++ supports a different function inheritance scheme when an overloaded and virtual function are involved. The function main() creates an instance for each of the three classes and invokes the various versions of the member function foo().

Nested Data Types

One problem plaguing C++ programmers is called *name space pollution*. This problem results from declaring too many identifiers, making the declaration of new ones likely to conflict with existing ones. In C++, classes can reduce this problem because C++ enables you to declare enumerated types, structures, and even classes that are nested in classes. Although these nested types remain accessible outside their host class, you need the class name to qualify them. Consequently, this approach reduces the chances of creating new names that conflict with others.

Example of Nested Types

Consider the following example of using nested types. Listing 11.4 contains the source code for the LST11_04.CPP program. The program declares a class that models dynamic stacks of unsigned integers. The stack uses single-linked lists as the underlying structure.

Listing 11.4. The source code for the LST11_04.CPP program.

```
// LST11_04.CPP
// Program demonstrates data types that are nested in a class

#include <iostream.h>
#include <string.h>
#include <conio.h>
```

```
class Stack
{
  public:
    // nested enumerated type
    enum boolean { false, true };
  protected:
    // nested structure
    struct StackNode {
        unsigned nodeData;
        StackNode *nextPtr;
    };
    unsigned height;   // height of stack
    StackNode *top; // pointer to the top of the stack
  public:
    Stack() : height(0), top(NULL) {}
    ~Stack() { clear(); }
    void push(unsigned);
    boolean pop(unsigned&);
    void clear();
};

void Stack::clear()
{
    unsigned x;
    while (pop(x)) /* do nothing */;
}

void Stack::push(unsigned x)
{
    StackNode *p;
    if (top) {
        p = new StackNode; // allocate new stack element
        p->nodeData = x;
     p->nextPtr = top;
     top = p;
    }
    else {
        top = new StackNode;
     top->nodeData = x;
     top->nextPtr = NULL;
    }
    height++;
}

Stack::boolean Stack::pop(unsigned& x)
{
    StackNode *p;
    if (height) {
        x = top->nodeData;
     p = top;
     top = top->nextPtr;
```

(continues)

Listing 11.4. Continued

```
            delete p; // deallocate stack node
            height--;
            return true;
        }
        else
          return false;
    }

    main()
    {
      Stack::boolean ok;
      Stack intStk;

      clrscr();
      for (unsigned x = 1; x < 7; x++) {
        cout << "Pushing " << x << " into the stack\n";
        intStk.push(x);
      }
      cout << "\nPopping off data from integer stack\n\n";
      ok = intStk.pop(x);
      while (ok) {
        cout << x << "\n";
        ok = intStk.pop(x);
      }
      return 0;
    }
```

The class Stack declares two nested types:

■ The StackNode structure, which contains two data members, nodeData
  and nextPtr. The nodeData member stores a list element (emulating a
  stack element). The nextPtr member is the pointer to the next list node.

■ The enumerated type boolean. For the sake of demonstration, this example declares the boolean type as a nested type rather than a global
  type. By contrast, the class implementation does not require using the
  StackNode structure outside the class (that is, a parameter in a member
  function uses that structure type).

The class Stack declares a set of data members, a constructor, a destructor,
and a set of member functions. These functions support the basic stack operations, such as pushing and popping data, and clearing the stack. These

member functions use the nested types to support the various operations. Here are two interesting pieces of code:

- The definition of the `pop()` member function uses the fully qualified name of the nested boolean type:

```
Stack::boolean Stack::pop(unsigned& x)
```

- The function `main()` declares the boolean variable `ok`, again by using the fully qualified name of the nested boolean type:

```
Stack::boolean ok;
```

The test program performs the trivial tasks of pushing and popping data into and off the stack. The following output is the product of the program in listing 11.4:

```
Pushing 1 into the stack
Pushing 2 into the stack
Pushing 3 into the stack
Pushing 4 into the stack
Pushing 5 into the stack
Pushing 6 into the stack

Popping off data from integer stack

6
5
4
3
2
1

Press any key to end the program...
```

Friend Classes

Just as C++ supports friend functions and friend operators, it also supports friend classes. C++ enables you to specify an across-the-board friendship between two classes.

Declaring a Friend Class

The syntax for declaring a friend class is

```
class className : [public] parentClass
{
     friend class befriendedClass;
     <private members>
     <protected members>
     <public members>
};
```

The *befriendedClass* is the class that becomes a friend to the class
className.

Example:

In this example, the class `Matrix` is a friend of class `Array`. This friendship is used to expand and contract the instances of class `Array` in the
functions `Matrix::storeRow()` and `Matrix::storeCol()`.

```
class Array
{
     friend class Matrix;

     protected:
          unsigned maxSize;
          double* arrPtr;
     public:
          Array(unsigned arrSize);
          ~Array();
          double& operator[](unsigned index);
          unsigned getSize() const;
};

class Matrix
{
     protected:
          unsigned maxRows;
          unsigned maxCols;
          double* matPtr;
     public:
          Matrix(unsigned numRows,
                    unsigned numCols);
          ~Matrix();
          unsigned getRows() const;
```

```
                        unsigned getCols() const;
                        double& operator()(unsigned row,
                                           unsigned col);
                        boolean storeCol(Array& arr,
                                         unsigned col);
                        boolean recallCol(Array& arr,
                                          unsigned col);
                        boolean storeRow(Array& arr,
                                         unsigned row);
                        boolean recallRow(Array& arr,
                                          unsigned row);
        };
```

Many C++ programmers have mixed feelings about using friend classes. Conceptually, a good class design should determine a safe interface with other classes, such that there is no need for using class friendship. I have had the opportunity to code two versions of the same set of classes: one using friendship and the other without such an access privilege. My conclusion is that you should use friendship between classes only to achieve significant increase in application speed—using the access member functions of a class can add significant overhead. To bypass that overhead, use friendship between classes.

Example of Friend Classes

Consider an example that puts class friendship to work. Listing 11.5 contains the source code for the LST11_05.CPP program. The program performs simple manipulation of numerical arrays and matrices.

Listing 11.5. The source code for the LST11_05.CPP program.

```
// LST11_05.CPP
// Program demonstrates friend classes

#include <iostream.h>
#include <string.h>
#include <conio.h>

const unsigned MIN_SIZE = 3;
const unsigned MIN_ROWS = 2;
const unsigned MIN_COLS = 2;

class Array
{
    // declare that class Matrix is a friend
    friend class Matrix;
```

(continues)

Listing 11.5. Continued

```
      protected:
        double *dataPtr;
        unsigned size;

      public:
        Array(unsigned Size = MIN_SIZE)
          { dataPtr = new double[size = Size]; }
        ~Array() { delete [] dataPtr; }
        unsigned getSize() const { return size; }
        double& operator [](unsigned index)
          { return *(dataPtr + index); }
  };

  class Matrix
  {
      protected:
        double *dataPtr;
        unsigned maxRows;
        unsigned maxCols;

      public:
        Matrix(unsigned Rows = MIN_ROWS,
               unsigned Cols = MIN_COLS) :
          maxRows(Rows), maxCols(Cols)
          { dataPtr = new double[Rows * Cols]; }
        ~Matrix() { delete [] dataPtr; }
        unsigned getMaxRows() const { return maxRows; }
        unsigned getMaxCols() const { return maxCols; }
        double& operator ()(unsigned row, unsigned col)
          { return *(dataPtr + row + col * maxRows); }
        void copyRow(Array& arr, unsigned row);
  };

  void Matrix::copyRow(Array& arr, unsigned row)
  {
    // delete array and re-create it to fit maxCols elements
    delete [] arr.dataPtr;
    arr.size = maxCols;
    arr.dataPtr = new double[arr.size];
    for (unsigned col = 0; col < maxRows; col++)
      arr[col] = *(dataPtr + row + col * maxRows);
  }

  main()
  {
    const unsigned ARR_SIZE = 5;
    const unsigned ROWS = 3;
    const unsigned COLS = 3;
    unsigned row, col;

    Array ar(ARR_SIZE);
    Matrix mat(ROWS, COLS);

    clrscr();
    // assign values to array ar
    for (unsigned i = 0; i < ar.getSize(); i++)
```

```
      ar[i] = 2.5 + i * i;

   // assign values to matrix at
   for (row = 0; row < mat.getMaxRows(); row++)
     for (col = 0; col < mat.getMaxCols(); col++)
       mat(row, col) = 5.5 + row + 10 * col;

   cout << "Array ar contains the following elements:\n\n";
   for (i = 0; i < ar.getSize(); i++)
     cout << "ar[" << i << "] = " << ar[i] << "\n";
   cout << "\nPress any key to continue..."; getch();

   clrscr();
   cout << "Matrix mat contains the following elements:\n\n";
   for (row = 0; row < mat.getMaxRows(); row++)
     for (col = 0; col < mat.getMaxCols(); col++)
       cout << "mat[" << row << "," << col << "] = "
            << mat(row, col) << "\n";
   cout << "\nPress any key to continue...";
   getch();

   // copy row 0 of matrix mat into array ar
   mat.copyRow(ar, 0);
   clrscr();
   cout << "Array ar contains the following elements:\n\n";
   for (i = 0; i < ar.getSize(); i++)
     cout << "ar[" << i << "] = " << ar[i] << "\n";
   return 0;
}
```

The program declares two classes, Array and Matrix. These classes are somewhat similar. The class Array is the same one presented in listing 11.5. Class Matrix is designed to resemble class Array. Class Matrix is designated as a friend of class Array by the appearance of the following declaration in class Array:

```
   friend class Matrix;
```

Notice that this example uses the operator () (which is called the *iterator* operator in C++) to act as an extended version of the operator []. Why use the operator () to access the element of a matrix? The operator [] can accept only one parameter, which must have an integer compatible type. By contrast, the operator () can take any number and any type of parameters. The operator (), therefore, is suitable for indexing matrices and other multidimensional arrays.

The class Matrix has two special member functions, copyRow() and copyCol(). These functions, as their names suggest, copy matrix rows and columns into the Array-typed reference parameter arr. These functions resize the array ar to match the size of a row or column. This process is possible only by making class Matrix a friend of class Array. This relationship enables the member functions of class Matrix to access the data members of class Array, dataPtr, and size, to perform the required operations.

The main() function performs the following tasks:

1. Declares the instance ar of class Array. The array stores five elements.

2. Declares the instance mat of class Matrix. The matrix contains three rows and three columns.

3. Assigns values to the array ar.

4. Assigns values to matrix mat.

5. Displays the elements of array ar.

6. Displays the elements of matrix mat.

7. Copies row 0 of the matrix mat into the array.

8. Displays the new elements of array ar.

Multiple Inheritance

C++ supports two types of class inheritance: single inheritance and *multiple inheritance*. Under single inheritance, a class has one and only one parent class. By contrast, under multiple inheritance, a class can have multiple parent classes.

Multiple inheritance is perhaps the most controversial feature of C++. Many computer scientists and programmers feel that multiple inheritance is a recipe for disaster. They regard containment (that is, declaring classes which contain data members that are themselves instances of other classes) as a much better and safer alternative to multiple inheritance.

Multiple inheritance, like containment, builds on the *HasA* notion. This notion defines the class as containing the parent classes instead of refining them. For example, you can model an airplane by creating classes for the different components—the engine, the wings, the wheels, the fuel system, the hydraulic system, and so on. Then you create a class that models the airplane by using multiple inheritance to inherit from all the components. This scheme applies the *HasA* notion and not the *IsA* notion—an airplane is not a type of wing, or an engine, or any other component. Instead, an airplane has a wing, has engines, and has the other components.

Declaring a Class Using Multiple Inheritance
The syntax for declaring a class using multiple inheritance is

```
class className : [public][virtual] parent1,
                  [public][virtual] parent2, ...
{

    private:
        <private data members>
        <private member functions>

    protected:
        <protected data members>
        <protected member functions>

    public:
        <public data members>
        <public member functions>
};
```

Example:
```
class Array
{
    protected:
        double *arrPtr;
        unsigned maxSize;
    public:
        Array(unsigned theMaxSize);
        ~Array();
        // other member functions
};

class Matrix
{
    protected:
        double *matPtr;
        unsigned maxRows;
        unsigned maxCols;
    public:
        Matrix(unsigned theMaxRows,
               unsigned theMaxCols);
        ~Matrix();
        // other member functions
```

(continues)

```
(continued)
    };

    class SimultEquations : public Matrix,
                            public Array
    {
        public:
            SimultEquations(unsigned theMaxRows,
                            unsigned theMaxCols);
            ~SimultEquations();
            solve();
    };
```

The keyword public works just as with single inheritance class derivation. The keyword virtual is needed for the parent classes that share a common ancestor class.

Example of Multiple Inheritance

The following short example uses multiple inheritance. Listing 11.6 contains source code for the LST11_06.CPP program.

Listing 11.6. The source code for the LST11_06.CPP program.

```
// LST11_06.CPP
// Program demonstrates multiple inheritance

#include <stdio.h>
#include <string.h>
#include <conio.h>

const SCREEN_CHARS = 2000;

class Cursor
{
  public:
    Cursor() {}
    void Gotoxy(int x, int y) { gotoxy(x, y); }
    void ClrScr() { clrscr(); }
    void ClrEol() { clreol(); }
    int WhereX() const { return wherex(); }
    int WhereY() const { return wherey(); }
    void pressAnyKey(const char* msg);
};

class String
{
```

```
      protected:
        char s[SCREEN_CHARS];

      public:
        String() { s[0] = '\0'; }
        String(const char* str) { strcpy(s, str); }
        char* getString() { return s; }
        void setString(const char* str)
          { strcpy(s, str); }
        void prependString(const char* str);
        void appendString(const char* str) { strcat(s, str); }
        int getLen() const { return strlen(s); }
};

class Screen : public Cursor, public String
{
    public:
      Screen() { ClrScr(); }
      void prompt(const char* msg, int x, int y);
      void display(int x, int y);
};

void Cursor::pressAnyKey(const char* msg)
{
  printf("%s", msg);
  getch();
}

void String::prependString(const char* str)
{
  char ss[SCREEN_CHARS];
  strcpy(ss, str);
  strcat(ss, s);
  strcpy(s, ss);
}

void Screen::prompt(const char* msg, int x, int y)
{
  char str[SCREEN_CHARS];
  Gotoxy(x, y);
  printf("%s", msg);
  gets(str);
  setString(str);
}

void Screen::display(int x, int y)
{
  char str[SCREEN_CHARS];
  Gotoxy(x, y);
  printf("%s", getString());
}

main()
{
  Screen scrn;
```

(continues)

Listing 11.6. continued

```
    scrn.prompt("Enter your name: ", 5, 7);
    scrn.prependString("Hello ");
    scrn.appendString(". How are you?");
    scrn.display(5, 10);
    scrn.Gotoxy(5, 22);
    scrn.pressAnyKey("Press any key to end the program...");
    return 0;
}
```

Listing 11.6 declares the following classes:

- Class `Cursor` models a screen cursor. The class has no data members and declares a default constructor as well as a set of member functions. The member functions perform common operations such as clearing the screen, clearing to the end of a line, getting the cursor location, and pausing with a message. Most of the functions are wrappers (that is, simple shells) for functions prototyped in the CONIO.H header file.

- Class `String` models screen text. The class declares a single data member that stores up to 2,000 characters (a screenful of text). The class declares two constructors and a set of simple string-manipulating member functions.

- Class `Screen` models a screen that has a cursor and text. The class uses multiple inheritance to inherit members from classes `Cursor` and `String`. The class `Screen` declares two member functions, `prompt()` and `display()`. The function `prompt()` gets a string using a prompting message that appears in a specified screen location. The function `display()` shows the contents of the inherited members at a specific screen location.

The `main()` function simply prompts you for your name and then uses your input to display a greeting message.

Summary

This chapter discussed the following advanced topics related to class hierarchy design:

- Declaring a class hierarchy enables you to derive classes from existing classes. The descendant classes inherit the members of their ancestor classes. C++ classes can override inherited member functions by defining their own versions. If you override a nonvirtual function, you can declare the new version using a different parameter list. By contrast, you cannot alter the parameter list of an inherited virtual function.

■ Virtual member functions enable your classes to support polymorphic behavior. Such behavior offers a response that is suitable for each class in a hierarchy. After you declare a virtual function, you can override it only with a virtual function in a descendant class. All versions of a virtual function in a class hierarchy must have the same signature.

■ Abstract classes empower you to specify the signature of important functions in a class hierarchy. This feature combines virtual functions and a special syntax to inform the compiler that the class contains abstract functions.

■ Overloaded member functions and operators enable a class to support more abstract expressions and statements. The various versions of an overloaded function or operator enable to you to specify various combinations of valid arguments.

■ Nested data types can appear in class declarations. These types include enumerated types, structures, and even classes. Nested types represent a vehicle for limiting the problem of name space pollution. You can refer to a nested type outside its class, but you need to qualify it with the name of the host class.

■ Friend classes have the privilege of accessing all the data members of a befriended class. Such a relation enables the friend class to quickly and flexibly alter instances of the befriended classes. Such instances typically are parameters that appear in the member functions of the befriended class.

■ Multiple inheritance is a scheme that enables you to derive a class from multiple parent classes. The descendant class has access to the various members of the parent classes.

Chapter 12

Stream File I/O

This chapter introduces file I/O operations using the C++ stream library. Although the STDIO.H library in C has been standardized by the ANSI C committee, the committee has not standardized the C++ stream library. You have a choice of using file I/O functions in the STDIO.H file or those in the C++ stream library. Each of these two I/O libraries offers a lot of power and flexibility. To learn more about the C++ stream library, consult a C++ language reference book, such as Stanley Lippman's C++ *Primer*, Second Edition, published by Addison-Wesley.

This chapter presents basic and practical operations that enable you to read and write data to files. In this chapter, you learn about the following topics:

- Common stream I/O functions

- Sequential stream I/O for text

- Sequential stream I/O for binary data

- Random-access stream I/O for binary data

The C++ Stream Library

The C++ stream I/O library is composed of a hierarchy of classes that are declared in several header files. The IOSTREAM.H header file that has been used to this point in this book is only one of these header files. Other files include IO.H, ISTREAM.H, OSTREAM.H, IFSTREAM.H, OFSTREAM.H, and FSTREAM.H. The IO.H header file declares low-level classes and identifiers. The ISTREAM.H and OSTREAM.H files support the basic input and output stream classes. The IOSTREAM.H combines the operations of the classes in the ISTREAM.H and OSTREAM.H header files. Similarly, the IFSTREAM.H and OFSTREAM.H files support the basic file input and output stream classes. The FSTREAM.H file combines the operations of the classes in the IFSTREAM.H and OFSTREAM.H header files.

In addition to the previously mentioned header files, C++ has stream library files that offer even more specialized stream I/O. The C++ ANSI committee should define the standard stream I/O library and end any confusion regarding which classes and header files are part of the standard stream library.

Common Stream I/O Functions

This section presents stream I/O functions that are common to both sequential and random-access I/O. These functions are detailed in the following list:

- *The* `open()` *function.* This function enables you to open a file stream for input, output, append, and both input and output operations. This function also enables you to specify whether the related I/O is binary or text. The declaration of the `open()` function is

```
void open(const char* filename,
          int mode,
          int m = filebuf::openprot);
```

The parameter `filename` specifies the name of the file to open. The parameter `mode` indicates the I/O mode. The following list contains arguments for parameter `mode` that are exported by the IO.H header file:

`in`	Open stream for input
`out`	Open stream for output
`ate`	Set stream pointer to the end of the file
`app`	Open stream for append mode
`trunc`	Truncate file size to 0 if it already exists
`nocreate`	Raise an error if the file does not already exist
`noreplace`	Raise an error if the file already exists
`binary`	Open in binary mode

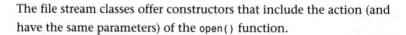 The file stream classes offer constructors that include the action (and have the same parameters) of the `open()` function.

- *The* `close()` *function.* This function closes the stream. The function takes no arguments and is declared as follows:

```
void close();
```

- The set of basic functions that check the error status of stream operations. The following functions are included in this set:

The `good()` function returns a nonzero value if there is no error in a stream operation. The declaration of the `good()` function is

```
int good();
```

The fail() function returns a nonzero value if there is an error in a stream operation. The declaration of the fail() function is

```
int fail();
```

The overloaded operator ! is applied to a stream instance to determine the error status.

The C++ stream libraries offer additional functions to set and query other aspects and types of stream errors.

Sequential Text Stream I/O

The functions and operators involved in sequential text I/O are simple. You have been exposed to most of these functions in earlier chapters. The functions and operators include

- The stream extractor operator, <<, which writes strings and characters to a stream.

- The stream inserter operator, >>, which reads characters from a stream.

- The getline() function, which reads strings from a stream. The declaration of the overloaded getline() function is

```
istream& getline(signed char* buffer,
                 int size,
                 char delimiter = '\n');

istream& getline(unsigned char* buffer,
                 int size,
                 char delimiter = '\n');
```

The parameter buffer is a pointer to the string receiving the characters from the stream. The parameter size specifies the maximum number of characters to read. The parameter delimiter specifies the delimiting character that causes the string input to stop before reaching the number of characters specified by parameter size. The parameter delimiter has the default argument of '\n'.

Example of Sequential I/O

The simple program in this example reads a text file, replaces the occurrences of a specific character in that file, and writes the output to a new file. Listing 12.1 shows the source code for the LST12_01.CPP program.

Listing 12.1. The source code for the LST12_01.CPP program.

```cpp
// LST12_01.CPP
// Program demonstrates sequential stream file I/O

#include <fstream.h>
#include <conio.h>

enum boolean { false, true };

main()
{
  const unsigned NAME_SIZE = 64;
  const unsigned LINE_SIZE = 128;

  fstream fin, fout;
  char inFile[NAME_SIZE + 1], outFile[NAME_SIZE + 1];
  char line[LINE_SIZE + 1];
  char findChar, replChar;
  unsigned i;
  boolean ok;

  clrscr();

  do {
    ok = true;
    cout << "Enter input file: ";
    cin.getline(inFile, NAME_SIZE); cout << '\n';
    fin.open(inFile, ios::in);
    if (!fin) {
      cout << "Cannot open file " << inFile << "\n\n";
      ok = false;
    }
  } while (!ok);

  do {
    ok = true;
    cout << "Enter output file: ";
    cin.getline(outFile, NAME_SIZE); cout << '\n';
    fout.open(outFile, ios::out);
    if (!fout) {
      cout << "File " << inFile << " is invalid\n\n";
      ok = false;
    }
  } while (!ok);

  cout << "\nEnter character to find: ";
  cin >> findChar;
  cout << "\nEnter character to replace: ";
  cin >> replChar;
  cout << "\n";

  // loop to replace the characters
  while (fin.getline(line, LINE_SIZE)) {
    for (i = 0; line[i] != '\0'; i++)
      if (line[i] == findChar)
```

```
        line[i] = replChar;
      // write line to the output file
      fout << line << "\n";
      // echo updated line to the screen
      cout << line << "\n";
    }
    // close streams
    fin.close();
    fout.close();
    return 0;
}
```

This program declares no classes, but instead focuses on using file streams to input and output text. The main() function performs the following relevant tasks:

1. Declares the input and output file streams, fin and fout.

2. Clears the screen and prompts you to enter the input file name. The function uses a do-while loop to validate your input and to carry out the following subtasks:

■ Setting the flag ok to true.

■ Displaying the prompting message.

■ Getting your input using the getline() function. Here the loop uses the getline() function with the standard input stream, cin.

■ Opening the input file stream, fin, using the function open(). The arguments for the function open() are the name of the input file and the expression ios::in, which specifies input mode only.

■ Using the overloaded operator ! to test whether the stream was successfully opened. If not, the loop displays an error message and assigns false to the variable ok.

3. Clears the screen and prompts you to enter the output file name. The function uses a do-while loop to validate your input in a manner similar to step 2. Notice that in this case, the stream function open() has the arguments outFile (the name of the output file) and ios::out (the expression that specifies output mode only).

4. Prompts you to enter the character to find.

5. Prompts you to enter the replacement character.

6. Uses a `while` loop to process the input lines by performing the following subtasks:

- Reading a line from the input file stream. This subtask applies the `getline()` function to the stream `fin`.

- Scanning the characters of the line read to locate and replace the characters that match the character in variable `findChar`.

- Writing the updated line to the output file stream, `fout`.

- Echoing the updated line to the standard output stream, `cout`.

7. Closes the input and output file streams.

Sequential Binary File Stream I/O

The C++ stream library offers the following stream functions for sequential binary file stream I/O:

- The function `write()` sends multiple bytes to an output stream. The overloaded function has the following declarations:

```
ostream& write(const signed char* buff, int num);
ostream& write(const unsigned char* buff, int num);
```

The parameter `buff` is the pointer to the buffer that contains the data to be sent to the output stream. The parameter `num` indicates the number of bytes in the buffer that are sent to the stream.

- The function `read()` receives multiple bytes from an input stream. The overloaded function has the following declarations:

```
istream& read(signed char* buff, int num);
istream& read(unsigned char* buff, int num);
```

The parameter `buff` is the pointer to the buffer that receives the data from the input stream. The parameter `num` indicates the number of bytes to read from the stream.

Example of Sequential Binary I/O

The following program example performs sequential binary stream I/O. Listing 12.2 shows the source code for the LST12_02.CPP program. This program declares a class that models dynamic numerical arrays. The stream I/O operations enable the program to read and write both the individual array elements and an entire array in binary files.

Listing 12.2. The source code for the LST12_02.CPP program.

```
// LST12_02.CPP
// Program demonstrates sequential binary file I/O

#include <fstream.h>
#include <conio.h>

const unsigned MIN_SIZE = 10;
const double BAD_VALUE = -1.0e+30;
enum boolean { false, true };

class Array
{
   protected:
     double *dataPtr;
     unsigned size;
     double badIndex;

   public:
     Array(unsigned Size = MIN_SIZE);
     ~Array() { delete [] dataPtr; }
     unsigned getSize() const { return size; }
     double& operator [](unsigned index)
        { return (index < size) ? *(dataPtr + index)
                                : badIndex; }
     boolean writeElem(fstream& os, unsigned index);
     boolean readElem(fstream& is, unsigned index);
     boolean writeArray(const char* filename);
     boolean readArray(const char* filename);
};

Array::Array(unsigned Size)
{
  size = (Size < MIN_SIZE) ? MIN_SIZE : Size;
  badIndex = BAD_VALUE;
  dataPtr = new double[size];
}

boolean Array::writeElem(fstream& os, unsigned index)
{
   if (index < size) {
     os.write((unsigned char*)(dataPtr + index),
              sizeof(double));
     return (os.good()) ? true : false;
   }
   else
     return false;
}

boolean Array::readElem(fstream& is, unsigned index)
{
```

(continues)

Listing 12.2. Continued

```cpp
        if (index < size) {
          is.read((unsigned char*)(dataPtr + index),
                sizeof(double));
          return (is.good()) ? true : false;
        }
        else
          return false;
    }

boolean Array::writeArray(const char* filename)
{
    fstream f(filename, ios::out | ios::binary);

    if (f.fail())
      return false;
    f.write((unsigned char*) &size, sizeof(size));
    f.write((unsigned char*)dataPtr, size * sizeof(double));
    f.close();
    return (f.good()) ? true : false;
}

boolean Array::readArray(const char* filename)
{
    fstream f(filename, ios::in | ios::binary);
    unsigned sz;

    if (f.fail())
      return false;
    f.read((unsigned char*) &sz, sizeof(sz));
    // need to expand the array
    if (sz != size) {
      delete [] dataPtr;
      dataPtr = new double[sz];
      size = sz;
    }
    f.read((unsigned char*)dataPtr, size * sizeof(double));
    f.close();
    return (f.good()) ? true : false;
}

main()
{
  const unsigned SIZE1 = 10;
  const unsigned SIZE2 = 20;
  Array ar1(SIZE1), ar2(SIZE1), ar3(SIZE2);
  fstream f("ar1.dat", ios::out | ios::binary);

  clrscr();
  // assign values to array ar1
  for (unsigned i = 0; i < ar1.getSize(); i++)
    ar1[i] = 10 * i;
  // assign values to array ar3
  for (i = 0; i < SIZE2; i++)
```

```
      ar3[i] = i;
    cout << "Array ar1 has the following values:\n";
    for (i = 0; i < ar1.getSize(); i++)
      cout << ar1[i] << "  ";
    cout << "\n\n";
    // write elements of array ar1 to the stream
    for (i = 0; i < ar1.getSize(); i++)
      ar1.writeElem(f, i);
    f.close();
    // reopen the stream for input
    f.open("ar1.dat", ios::in | ios::binary);
    for (i = 0; i < ar1.getSize(); i++)
      ar2.readElem(f, i);
    f.close();
    // display the elements of array ar2
    cout << "Array ar2 has the following values:\n";
    for (i = 0; i < ar2.getSize(); i++)
      cout << ar2[i] << "  ";
    cout << "\n\n";
    // display the elements of array ar3
    cout << "Array ar3 has the following values:\n";
    for (i = 0; i < ar3.getSize(); i++)
      cout << ar3[i] << "  ";
    cout << "\n\n";
    // write the array ar3 to file AR3.DAT
    ar3.writeArray("ar3.dat");
    // read the array ar1 from file AR3.DAT
    ar1.readArray("ar3.dat");
    // display the elements of array ar1
    cout << "Array ar1 now has the following values:\n";
    for (i = 0; i < ar1.getSize(); i++)
      cout << ar1[i] << "  ";
    return 0;
  }
```

This program declares a version of class Array that resembles versions presented in the preceding chapter. This version differs from previous versions in that it includes the following four member functions to perform sequential binary file stream I/O:

■ The writeElem() function writes a single array element to an output stream:

```
    boolean writeElem(fstream& os, unsigned index);
```

The parameter os represents the output stream. The parameter index specifies the array element to write. The writeElem() function returns true if the argument for the index is valid and if the stream output proceeds without any error. After the writeElem() function writes an array element, the internal stream pointer advances to the next location.

■ The readElem() function reads a single array element from an input stream:

```
boolean readElem(fstream& is, unsigned index);
```

The parameter is represents the input stream. The parameter index specifies the array element to read. The readElem() function returns true if the argument for the index is valid and if the stream input proceeds without any error. After the readElem() function reads an array element, the internal stream pointer advances to the next location.

The functions writeElem() and readElem() permit the same class instance to write and read data elements from multiple streams.

■ The writeArray() function writes the entire elements of the array to a binary file:

```
boolean writeArray(const char* filename);
```

The parameter filename specifies the name of the output file. The function opens an output stream and writes the value of the data member size and then writes the elements of the dynamic array. The writeArray() function returns true if it successfully writes the array to the stream; otherwise, the function yields false. The function opens a local output stream using the stream function open() and supplies it with the file name and I/O mode arguments. The I/O mode argument is the expression ios::out ¦ ios::binary. This expression specifies that the stream is opened for binary output only. The function makes two calls to the stream function write(): the first to write the data member size, and the second to write the elements of the dynamic array.

■ The readArray() function reads the entire elements of the array from a binary file:

```
boolean readArray(const char* filename);
```

The parameter filename specifies the name of the input file. The function opens an input stream and reads the value of the data member size and then reads the elements of the dynamic array. The readArray() function returns true if it successfully reads the array to the stream; otherwise, the function yields false. The function opens a local input stream using the stream function open() and supplies it with the file name and I/O mode arguments. The I/O mode argument is the expression ios::in ¦ ios::binary, which specifies that the stream is opened for binary input only. The function makes two calls to the stream function `read()`: the first to read the data member size, and the second to read the elements of the dynamic array.

Another feature of function `readArray()` is that it resizes the instance of class `Array` to accommodate the data from the binary file. This means that the dynamic array accessed by the class instance can either shrink or expand, depending on the size of the array stored on file.

These four member functions indicate that the program performs two types of sequential binary stream I/O. The first type of I/O, implemented in functions `readElem()` and `writeElem()`, involves items that have the same data type. The second type of I/O, implemented in functions `readArray()` and `writeArray()`, involves items that have different data types.

The `main()` function performs the following relevant tasks:

1. Declares three instances of class `Array`: ar1, ar2, and ar3. The first two instances have the same dynamic array size, whereas instance ar3 has a larger dynamic array than the other two.

2. Declares the file stream f and opens it (using a stream constructor) to access file AR1.DAT in binary output mode.

3. Assigns values to the instances ar1 and ar3.

4. Displays the elements of instance ar1.

5. Writes the elements of array ar1 to the output file stream f. This task uses a loop that calls the `writeElem()` function and supplies it with the arguments f (the file stream) and i (the loop control variable).

6. Closes the output file stream.

7. Opens the file stream f to access the data file AR1.DAT. This time, the function specifies a binary input mode.

8. Reads the elements of instance ar2 (which has not yet been assigned any values) from the input file stream f. This task uses a loop that calls the `readElem()` function and supplies it with the arguments f (the file stream) and i (the loop control variable).

9. Closes the input file stream.

10. Displays the elements of instance ar2. These elements match those of instance ar1.

11. Displays the elements of instance ar3.

12. Writes the entire instance ar3 using the function writeArray(). The argument for the writeArray() function call is the file name AR3.DAT.

13. Reads the array in file AR3.DAT into instance ar1. This task uses the readArray() function and supplies it the argument for the file name AR3.DAT.

14. Displays the new elements of instance ar1.

A sample session with the program in listing 12.2 produces the following output:

```
Array ar1 has the following values:
0  10  20  30  40  50  60  70  80  90

Array ar2 has the following values:
0  10  20  30  40  50  60  70  80  90

Array ar3 has the following values:
0  1  2  3  4  5  6  7  8  9  10  11  12  13  14  15  16  17  18  19

Array ar1 now has the following values:
0  1  2  3  4  5  6  7  8  9  10  11  12  13  14  15  16  17  18  19
```

Random-Access File Stream I/O

Random-access file stream operations also use the stream functions read() and write(), presented in the preceding section. The stream library offers a set of stream-seeking functions to enable you to move the stream pointer to any valid location. The function seekg() is one such function. This overloaded function has the following declaration:

```
istream& seekg(long pos);
istream& seekg(long pos, seek_dir dir);
```

The parameter pos in the first version specifies the absolute byte position in the stream. In the second version, the parameter pos specifies a relative offset based on the argument for parameter dir.

The arguments for the latter parameter are shown in the following list:

`ios::beg`	From the beginning of the file
`ios::cur`	From the current position of the file
`ios::end`	From the end of the file

Example of Random-Access I/O

The example in this section uses random-access file stream I/O. The LST12_03 program implements a virtual (that is, disk-based) array. Accessing the different array elements requires random-access I/O. Listing 12.3 shows the source code for the LST12_03.CPP program.

Listing 12.3. The source code for the LST12_03.CPP program.

```cpp
// LST12_03.CPP
// Program demonstrates random-access binary file I/O

#include <fstream.h>
#include <conio.h>
#include <stdlib.h>

const unsigned MIN_SIZE = 5;
const double BAD_VALUE = -1.0e+30;
enum boolean { false, true };

class VmArray
{
   protected:
     fstream f;
     unsigned size;
     double badIndex;

   public:
     VmArray(unsigned Size, const char* filename);
     ~VmArray() { f.close(); }
     unsigned getSize() const { return size; }
     boolean writeElem(double x, unsigned index);
     boolean readElem(double& x, unsigned index);
     void Combsort();
};

VmArray::VmArray(unsigned Size, const char* filename)
{
   size = (Size < MIN_SIZE) ? MIN_SIZE : Size;
   badIndex = BAD_VALUE;
   f.open(filename, ios::in | ios::out | ios::binary);
   if (f.good()) {
     // fill the file stream with zeros
     double x = 0.0;
```

(continues)

Listing 12.3. Continued

```
      f.seekg(0);
      for (unsigned i = 0; i < size; i++)
        f.write((unsigned char*) &x, sizeof(double));
  }
}

boolean VmArray::writeElem(double x, unsigned index)
{
    if (index < size) {
      f.seekg(index * sizeof(double));
      f.write((unsigned char*)&x, sizeof(double));
      return (f.good()) ? true : false;
    }
    else
      return false;
}

boolean VmArray::readElem(double &x, unsigned index)
{
    if (index < size) {
      f.seekg(index * sizeof(double));
      f.read((unsigned char*)&x, sizeof(double));
      return (f.good()) ? true : false;
    }
    else
      return false;
}

void VmArray::Combsort()
{
    unsigned i, j, gap = size;
    boolean inOrder;
    double xi, xj;

    do {
      gap = gap * 8 / 11;
      gap = (gap < 1) ? 1 : gap;
      inOrder = true;
      for (i = 0, j = gap; i < (size - gap); i++, j++) {
        readElem(xi, i);
        readElem(xj, j);
        if (xi > xj) {
          inOrder = false;
          writeElem(xi, j);
          writeElem(xj, i);
        }
      }
    } while (!(inOrder && gap == 1));
}

main()
{
  VmArray ar(10, "ar.dat");
  double x;
```

```
    clrscr();
    // assign random values to array ar
    for (unsigned i = 0; i < ar.getSize(); i++) {
      x = (double) (1 + random(1000));
      ar.writeElem(x, i);
    }
    cout << "Unsorted array is\n";
    for (i = 0; i < ar.getSize(); i++) {
      ar.readElem(x, i);
      cout << x << ' ';
    }
    ar.Combsort(); // sort array
    cout << "\n\nSorted array is\n";
    for (i = 0; i < ar.getSize(); i++) {
      ar.readElem(x, i);
      cout << x << ' ';
    }
    return 0;
  }
```

The class VmArray models a disk-based dynamic array that stores all of its elements in a random-access binary file. Notice that the class declares an instance of class fstream and that there is no pointer to a dynamic array. The
class declares a constructor, a destructor, and a set of member functions.

The class constructor has two parameters: Size and filename. The parameter
Size specifies the size of the virtual array. The parameter filename names the
binary file that stores the elements of a class instance. The constructor opens
the stream f using the stream function open() and supplies the argument of
parameter filename and the I/O mode expression ios::in ¦ ios::out ¦
ios::binary. This expression specifies that the stream is opened for binary
input and output mode (that is, random-access mode). If the constructor
successfully opens the file stream, it fills the file with zeros. The class destructor performs the simple task of closing the file stream f.

The functions writeElem() and readElem() support the random access of array
elements. These functions use the stream function seekg() to position the
stream pointer at the appropriate array element. The writeElem() function
then calls the stream function write() to store an array element (supplied by
the parameter x). By contrast, the function readElem() calls the stream function read() to retrieve an array element (returned by the parameter x). Both
functions return boolean results that indicate the success of the I/O
operation.

The VmArray class also declares the Combsort() function to sort the elements of
the virtual array. This function uses the readElem() and writeElem() member

functions to access and swap the array elements.

The main() function performs the following relevant tasks:

1. Declares the instance ar, of class VmArray. This instance stores 10 elements in the binary file AR.DAT.

2. Assigns random values to the elements of instance ar. This task uses a loop that creates random numbers and assigns them to the local variable x. The loop then writes the value in x to the instance ar by calling the function writeElem(). The arguments for the call to writeElem() are x and i (i is the the loop control variable).

3. Displays the unsorted elements of instance ar.

4. Sorts the array by invoking the Combsort() member function.

5. Displays the sorted elements of instance ar.

The following output is from a sample session with the program in listing 12.3:

```
Unsorted array is
11 4 336 34 356 218 537 196 701 950

Sorted array is
4 11 34 196 218 336 356 537 701 950
```

Summary

This chapter gave you a brief introduction to the C++ stream I/O library. The chapter discussed the following topics:

■ Common stream I/O functions. These stream functions include open(), close(), good(), fail(), and the operator !. The function open(), as the name suggests, opens a file for stream I/O and supports alternate and multiple I/O modes. The function close() shuts down a file stream. The functions good() and fail() indicate the success or failure of a stream I/O operation.

■ Sequential stream I/O for text. C++ enables you to perform this kind of stream I/O using the operators << and >>, as well as the stream function getline(). The operator << can write characters and strings (as well as the other predefined data types). The operator >> is suitable for getting characters. The function `getline()` enables your applications to read strings from the keyboard or from a text file.

■ Sequential stream I/O for binary data, which uses the stream functions `write()` and `read()` to write and read data from any kind of variables.

■ Random-access stream I/O for binary data, which uses the `seekg()` function with the functions `read()` and `write()`. The `seekg()` function enables you to move the stream pointer to either absolute or relative byte locations in the stream.

Chapter 13

The C++ Exceptions

Borland C++ 4 introduces the *exceptions* language feature. This feature enables C++ programmers to better generate and handle run-time errors. The ANSI C++ Standards Committee has accepted the exceptions feature and is now writing the standards for this feature.

The name *exception* seems to have come from the notion that a run-time error causes a somewhat abnormal flow of program execution. This kind of execution is the *exception* and not the rule.

Overview of Exceptions

The C++ language uses the defensive programming approach inherited from its parent language, C. Other languages, such as Ada and even various Microsoft Basic implementations offer more sophisticated run-time error-handling. The new Borland C++ exception feature enables your program to *throw* (that is, to generate) an exception in one part (at run time) and have another part *catch* (that is, handle or deal with) that exception.

Borland C++ supports an exception-handling scheme that requires the following ingredients:

- Declaring one or more classes or structures that each represent a specific kind of exception
- Specifying which functions can throw what exceptions
- Declaring exception objects
- Throwing exceptions
- Catching exceptions of different kinds

This chapter looks at the exceptions feature as supported by Borland C++. In this chapter, you learn about the following topics:

- Overview of exceptions
- Declaring classes and structures that support exceptions
- Declaring which functions can throw exceptions
- Declaring exception objects
- Throwing exceptions
- Catching exceptions
- Managing unexpected exceptions
- Examples of declaring, throwing, and handling exceptions

The Exception Types

Borland C++ requires that you define a class or structure which represents a category of exceptions. Unlike most useful classes that you write, exception classes can be useful even if they have no members. Memberless exception classes utilize the class name mainly as a way to tag or label the exception category.

Declaring an Exception Class

The general syntax for declaring a class that represents an exception is:

```
class exceptionName {
[public:
   // declarations of public members]
[protected:
   // declarations of protected members]
[private:
   // declarations of private members]
};
```

Examples:

The following classes model common categories of errors:

```
class TCalculationError {};
class TFileException
{
  public:
    enum (FE_FileNotFound, FE_InvalidPath,
FE_DiskFull };
    enum FE_Error;
}
```

The class TCalculationError has no members and relies mainly on its name to identify the kind of error it represents. By contrast, the class TFileException declares a nested enumerated type and the data member FE_Error to identify the kinds of file I/O errors represented by this class.

Enabling Functions to Throw Exceptions

Borland C++ supports the following rules that govern the scope of throwing and catching exceptions:

- Within any function and member function you can throw and catch exceptions.

- Any function and member function can throw any kind of exception that is handled by other functions, unless you specify the kind of exceptions that can be thrown by the function.

- You can use special syntax to prevent a function or member function from throwing any kind of exception to other functions.

- You can use special syntax to specify which exceptions can be thrown by a function or member function to other functions.

Designating a Function's Exception-Throwing Capability

The syntax for enabling a function or member function to throw any kind of exception is:

```
returnType functionName([parameter_list]);
```

The syntax for preventing a function or member function from throwing any kind of exception is:

```
returnType functionName([parameter_list])
throw();
```

The syntax for enabling a function or member function to throw specific kinds of exceptions is:

```
returnType functionName([parameter_list])
throw(exception_type_list);
```

The *exception_type_list* is a comma-delimited list of exceptions that can be thrown by the function *functionName*() to other functions.

Examples:

```
// throw any exception
double Calculate();
// cannot throw any exception
char* ProcessString(char* Str) throw();

// throw one kind of exception
int ReadData(const char* Filename):
throw(TFileError);

// throw two kinds of exceptions
int InputData(const char* Filename)
throw(TFileError, TMemoryError);
```
(continues)

(continued)

The preceding declaration enables function `Calculate()` to throw any kind of exceptions. By contrast, the function `ProcessString()` cannot throw any kind of exception. The function `ReadData()` can throw only exceptions that have the type TFileError or descendants of that type. The function `InputData()` can throw exceptions of the types TFileError or TMemoryError, or the descendants of these two types.

Declaring Exception Objects

The exception classes and structures you declare identify the kinds of errors the classes and structures represent. A function handles a specific instance of an error type when a specific instance of the exception class or structure occurs. The function that detects an error condition throws an exception object (and not a class).

Throwing Exceptions

Borland C++ enables a function or member function use the `throw()` function to throw an exception. This function specifies the exception object to be thrown.

Throwing an Exception

The general syntax for throwing an exception is:

```
throw(exception_object);
```

The *exception_object* is an instance of a class or structure that models an exception.

Example:

```
class TFileError {};
TFileError FileError;

void ReadDataFile(const char* Filename)
{
    fstream f;
```

```
        if(!f.open(Filename, ios::in ¦ ios::binary))
            throw(FileError);
        else {
            ...
        }
    }
```

The preceding code shows that the function ReadDataFile() throws the exception object FileError if the function fails to open the input stream f. The exception is handled by the caller of function ReadDataFile().

Catching Exceptions

Borland C++ uses the try block to contain potentially offending code; further, the program uses one or more catch blocks to handle exceptions thrown in a statement inside the try block.

Writing *Try* and *Catch* Blocks

The general syntax for the try and catch blocks is:

```
try {
    // statements that may throw one or more kinds of
exceptions
}
catch(exceptionType1) {
    // statements that deal with the exceptionType1
type or error
}
catch(exceptionType2) {
    // statements that deal with the exceptionType2
type or error
}
...
catch(exceptionTypeN) {
    // statements that deal with the exceptionTypeN
type or error
}
catch(...) {
    // statements that handle all other kinds of excep-
tions
}
```

(continues)

(continued)

The catch(...) block is a catch-all block that handles exceptions not listed in the leading catch blocks. A try block may contain only the catch(...) block.

The try block may contain throw statements that directly throw exceptions handled by one of the catch blocks.

Example:

```
class TFileError {};
TFileError FileError;

class TMemoryError {};
TMemoryError MemoryError;

class TUserError {};
TUserError UserError;

void ProcessData()
{
...
  if (....)
    throw(FileError);
...
  if (....)
    throw(MemoryError);
...
  if (....)
    throw(UserError);
...
}

void main()
{
 try {
  ProcessData();
 }
 catch(TFileError)
 {
  cout << "File I/O error\n";
 }
 catch(TMemoryError)
 {

  cout << "Memory error\n";
 }
 catch(TUserError)
 {
```

```
     cout << "Logical error\n";
   }
   catch(...)
   {
     cout << "Unidentified error";
   }
   return 0;
   }
```

In the preceding example, function main() uses the try block that contains the call to function ProcessData(). The function ProcessData() can generate errors that are of the types TFileError, TMemoryError, and TUserError. The function main() has a set of catch blocks (including the catch(...) block) to handle various kinds of exceptions.

Examples

The following examples present two versions of a programming sample that implements a simple floating-point calculator. This calculator prompts you to enter the operands and operator. The program supports the basic four math operations plus the exponentiation (raising to power) that uses the character ^. The program performs the operation you request (if your input is valid) and displays the operands, operator, and the result. If your input is invalid, the program displays an error message. The program detects the following errors:

- Division by zero

- Invalid operator

- Raising a negative number to a power

The program prompts you for additional calculations. Listing 13.1 shows the source code for the LST13_01.CPP program.

Listing 13.1. The source code for the LST13_01.CPP program.

```
/*
  Program which illustrates using C++ exceptions
  to manage various kinds of run time errors
*/
```

(continues)

Listing 13.1. Continued

```cpp
#include <iostream.h>
#include <math.h>
#include <conio.h>

const BAD_RESULT = -1.0e+100;

class TOperatorException {};
TOperatorException InvalidOperatorError;

class TZeroDivisionException {};
TZeroDivisionException ZeroDivideError;

class TPowerToNegNumException {};
TPowerToNegNumException PowerOfNegNumError;

class TOperation
{
 public:
  TOperation();

  void SetOperand1(double x)
     { X = x; }
  void SetOperand2(double y)
     { Y = y; }
  void SetOperator(char op)
     { Op = op; }
  double Add()
     { return X + Y; }
  double Sub()
     { return X - Y; }
  double Mul()
     { return X * Y; }
  double Div() throw(TZeroDivisionException);
  double Power() throw(TPowerToNegNumException);
  double Calculate();

 protected:
     double X;
     double Y;
     char Op;
};

TOperation::TOperation()
{
  X = 0;
  Y = 0;
  Op = ' ';
}

double TOperation::Div()
      throw(TZeroDivisionException)
```

```
{
  if (Y != 0)
      return X / Y;
  else
      throw(ZeroDivideError);
}

double TOperation::Power()
     throw(TPowerToNegNumException)
{
  if (X < 0)
      throw(PowerOfNegNumError);
  else
      return  exp(log(X) * Y);
}

double TOperation::Calculate()
{
  double Z = BAD_RESULT;

  try {
      switch (Op) {
          case '+':
              Z = Add();
            break;

          case '-':
            Z = Sub();
            break;

          case '*':
            Z = Mul();
            break;

          case '/':
            Z = Div();
            break;

          case '^':
            Z = Power();
            break;

          default:
            throw(InvalidOperatorError);
      }
  }
  catch(TOperatorException)
  {
      cout << "Error: The operator '" << Op << "' is not valid";
  }
  catch(TZeroDivisionException)
  {
      cout << "Error: Attempt to divide by zero";
```

(continues)

Listing 13.1. Continued

```
    }
    catch (...)
    {
        cout << "Error: Attempt to raise power of a negative number";
    };
    return Z;
}

main()
{
  char answer, op;
  double x, y, z;
  TOperation Operation;

  do {
      cout << "\n\nEnter first operand : ";
      cin >> x;
      cout << "Enter second operand : ";
      cin >> y;
      cout << "Enter operator : ";
      cin >> op;
      cout << "\n\n";
      Operation.SetOperand1(x);
      Operation.SetOperand2(y);
      Operation.SetOperator(op);
      z = Operation.Calculate();
      if (z > BAD_RESULT) {
          cout << x << ' ' << op << ' '
                  << y << " = " << z << "\n";
      }
      cout << "\nWant to perform more calculations? (Y/N) ";
      answer = getche();
  } while (answer == 'Y' || answer == 'y');
  return 0;
}
```

Listing 13.1 declares the following exception classes:

■ The class TOperatorException that represents invalid operator errors.

■ The class TZeroDivisionException that supports the division-by-zero error.

■ The class TPowerToNegNumException that represents the errors generated by raising a negative number to a power. This error is related to the way the program calculates the power of a number.

The listing declares a global instance of each of the above classes. The listing also declares the class TOperation; the member functions of this class perform the following tasks:

- Assigning values to operands and operators (stored in the data members X, Y, and Op).

- Performing addition, multiplication, subtraction, division, and exponentiation.

- Managing the above mathematical operations.

The member functions DIV() and Power() throw the TZeroDivisionException and TPowerToNegNumException exceptions, respectively. For the sake of demonstration, the program in listing 13.1 declares that these functions only throw their respective exception types. When you examine the definitions of member functions DIV() and Power(), you notice that they contain throw statements that throw the exception objects ZeroDivideError and PowerOfNegNumError, respectively.

The definition of the member function Calculate() has a try block that contains a switch statement used to execute the requested operation. The try block is able to handle the exceptions thrown by member functions DIV() and Power(), as well as the one explicitly thrown by the throw statement in the default clause. The function Calculate() contains three catch blocks, including the catch(...) block. These blocks handle the three kinds of exceptions defined in the program. The example uses catch(...) for the purposes of demonstration; you can replace the catch(...) with catch(TPowerToNegNumException) without affecting how the program interacts with the user.

Listing 13.1 contains the function main(), that declares an instance of class TOperation. The function main() uses a do-while loop to prompt you for input. The function main() then sends the C++ messages SetOperand1, SetOperand2, SetOperator, and Calculate to the object Operation. The function examines the value in the variable z to determine if the requested operation was successfully carried out. The following example demonstrates a sample session with program LST13_01.EXE:

```
Enter first operand : 5
Enter second operand : 0  ·
Enter operator : /

Error: Attempt to divide by zero
Want to perform more calculations? (Y/N) y

Enter first operand : 5
Enter second operand : 3
Enter operator : ^

5 ^ 3 = 125
Want to perform more calculations? (Y/N) n
```

The program in listing 13.1 uses three separate exception classes to identify three kinds of errors. All of these exception classes are memberless. The next program uses a single exception class that has a string-type data member. This member stores the error messages that identify the type of error represented by the class. Listing 13.2 shows the source code for the LST13_02.CPP program.

Listing 13.2. The source code for the LST13_02.CPP program.

```
/*
  Program which illustrates using C++ exceptions
  to manage various kinds of run time errors
*/

#include <iostream.h>
#include <math.h>
#include <conio.h>
#include <string.h>

const BAD_RESULT = -1.0e+100;

class TOperationException
{
 public:
   TOperationException()
       { ErrMsg[0] = '\0'; }

   char ErrMsg[128];
};

TOperationException TheError;

class TOperation
{
```

```
 public:
  TOperation();

  void SetOperand1(double x)
      { X = x; }
  void SetOperand2(double y)
      { Y = y; }
  void SetOperator(char op)
      { Op = op; }

  double Add()
      { return X + Y; }
  double Sub()
      { return X - Y; }
  double Mul()
      { return X * Y; }
  double Div() throw(TOperationException);
  double Power() throw(TOperationException);
  double Calculate();

 protected:
     double X;
     double Y;
     char Op;
};

TOperation::TOperation()
{
  X = 0;
  Y = 0;
  Op = ' ';
}

double TOperation::Div()
      throw(TOperationException)
{
  if (Y != 0)
      return X / Y;
  else {
      strcpy(TheError.ErrMsg,
                "Error: Division by zero");
      throw(TheError);
  }
}

double TOperation::Power()
     throw(TOperationException)
{
  if (X < 0) {
      strcpy(TheError.ErrMsg,
           "Error: Invalid exponentiation");
      throw(TheError);
  }
```

(continues)

Listing 13.2. Continued

```
    else
        return  exp(log(X) * Y);
}


double TOperation::Calculate()
{
  double Z = BAD_RESULT;

  try {
      switch (Op) {
          case '+':
              Z = Add();
            break;

          case '-':
            Z = Sub();
            break;

          case '*':
            Z = Mul();
            break;

          case '/':
            Z = Div();
            break;

          case '^':
            Z = Power();
            break;

          default:
            strcpy(TheError.ErrMsg,
                       "Error: Invalid operator");
            throw(TheError);
      }
    }
  catch(TOperationException)
  {
      cout << TheError.ErrMsg;
  }
  return Z;
}

main()
{
  char answer, op;
  double x, y, z;
  TOperation Operation;
```

```
    do {
        cout << "\n\nEnter first operand : ";
        cin >> x;
        cout << "Enter second operand : ";
        cin >> y;
        cout << "Enter operator : ";
        cin >> op;
        cout << "\n\n";
        Operation.SetOperand1(x);
        Operation.SetOperand2(y);
        Operation.SetOperator(op);
        z = Operation.Calculate();
        if (z > BAD_RESULT) {
            cout << x << ' ' << op << ' '
                 << y << " = " << z << "\n";
        }
        cout << "\nWant to perform more calculations? (Y/N) ";
        answer = getche();
    } while (answer == 'Y' || answer == 'y');
    return 0;
}
```

The program in listing 13.2 declares the class TOperationException to support the various kinds of operational errors. The class declares a constructor and the data member ErrMsg. This member stores the error message that describes the various kinds of operational errors. The listing also declares the object TheError as an instance of class TOperationException. The declaration for class TOperationException in this program is similar to the declaration in listing 13.1. The difference between the two declarations is that member functions DIV() and Power(), as declared in listing 13.2, both throw the error type TOperationException.

The implementation of member function DIV() and Power() has changed in listing 13.2. The functions assign error message text to the ErrMsg data member of object TheError and then throw that object.

The implementation of member function Calculate() is shorter in listing 13.2 than in listing 13.1. The new version uses the single catch block to catch the object TheError. The statement in the catch block displays the contents of data member ErrMsg. Also notice that the default clause in member function Calculate() assigns an error message text to data member ErrMsg and then throws the object TheError.

The changes in the exception classes and class TOperation do not affect the code in function main().

A session with the program LST13_02.EXE is presented in this example:

```
Enter first operand : -5
Enter second operand : 2
Enter operator : ^

Error: Invalid exponentiation
Want to perform more calculations? (Y/N) y

Enter first operand : 5
Enter second operand : 2
Enter operator : *

5 * 2 = 10
Want to perform more calculations? (Y/N) n
```

Summary

This chapter presented the new Borland C++ exceptions features. You learned about the following topics:

- An overview of exceptions and the language components needed to support them.

- Declaring classes and structures that support exceptions as the first step in supporting exceptions. These classes and structures need not have data members to be useful; many kinds of exceptions can be implemented with memberless classes.

- How to restrict functions from throwing any or only specific exceptions. This restriction uses the keyword throw after the function's parameter list. If the keyword throw has an empty list, the associated function cannot throw any exceptions. By contrast, if the throw keyword lists one or more exception classes, the associated function can throw only exceptions of the listed types.

- Declaring exception objects (that is, instances of exception classes) to be thrown.

- Throwing exceptions by using the throw keyword that has an exception object as its single argument.

- Detecting and catching exceptions using the try block followed by one or more catch blocks. Each catch block states the exception class to handle. The special catch(...) block acts as a catch-all.

■ Examining two versions of a program that uses exceptions to handle errors involved in simple mathematical operations. The first version uses separate memberless exception classes to represent the various errors. The second version employs a single exception class with a data member. This class replaces the memberless exception classes in the first version.

Chapter 14

Using ObjectWindows Library

The ObjectWindows Hierarchy

Windows programs involve considerably more code than comparable MS-DOS programs. Using C programs to develop Windows applications dictates numerous lines of code that use the Windows API (Application Program Interface) functions. Using C++ to write these programs can decrease the size of the source code by employing a class hierarchy with descendant classes that inherit the operations of their parent classes. You can create such a C++ class library to encapsulate the calls to the various Windows API functions. Fortunately, Borland has performed this task for you. The *ObjectWindows library* (OWL) offers a versatile tool that assists you in crafting Windows applications. The ObjectWindows library succeeds in bringing together object-oriented and event-driven programming concepts; the library also illustrates how well these two programming disciplines work together.

The ObjectWindows library contains numerous descendant classes that inherit operations from their parent classes. The library uses both single- and multiple-inheritance to implement the various OWL classes. The presentation and discussion of the OWL classes is worthy of an entire book. For the purposes of this book, however, consider the following general categories of OWL classes:

- Module and application classes
- Window classes

This chapter presents various Windows programs that use the Object-Windows Library text editor program generated by the AppExpert utility. In this chapter, you learn about the following topics:

- A general overview of the ObjectWindows hierarchy
- Responding to Windows messages
- Sending Windows messages
- The user-defined messages
- Examples of OWL-based Windows programs

- Document and view classes

- Control classes

- Dialog box classes

- Graphics classes

- Printing classes

- Miscellaneous classes

The examples presented in this chapter include some OWL classes. For a complete discussion of OWL classes and information about programming Windows applications using the OWL classes, you can obtain a book such as Que's *Object-Oriented Programming with Borland C++ 4*.

Sending and Responding to Messages

Windows uses the object-oriented metaphor where objects communicate among themselves via messages. A diverse set of events, such as clicking the mouse button, pressing the keyboard, and manipulating windows, generates messages aimed at specific windows. The Windows system has a large set of predefined messages that manage the operations of windows, dialog boxes, controls, and other invisible items.

In addition to the Windows messages generated by the mouse and keyboard events, your Windows programs can explictly send messages using the SendMessage API function. The OWL class TWindow declares the member function SendMessage as a wrapper for the SendMessage API function. The declaration for the SendMessage member function is

```
inline LRESULT SendMessage(UINT msg, WPARAM wParam = 0,
                           LPARAM lParam = 0) const;
```

The parameter msg is the numeric code identifying the message sent by the member function. The parameters wParam and lParam supply additional information associated with the generated message. An example of using the SendMessage member function is

```
SendMessage(WM_CLOSE);
```

which closes a window.

The OWL classes use special groups of macros; these macros map the various categories of Windows messages onto the member functions that respond to these messages. To understand these macros, first examine the following code fragment:

```
class TMyWindow : public TWindow
{
 public:
      TMyWindow();
 protected:
      // handle left mouse button click
      void EvLButtonDown();
      // handle moving the window
      void EvMove(TPoint& clientOrigin);
      // handle painting the window
      void EvPaint()
      // handling exiting from the application
      void CmExit();
      // other member functions

      DECLARE_RESPONSE_TABLE(TMyWindow);
};

DEFINE_RESPONSE_TABLE1(TMyWindow, TWindow)
      EV_WM_LBUTTONDOWN,
       EV_WM_MOVE,
      EV_WM_PAINT,
      EV_COMMAND(CM_EXIT, CmExit),
END_RESPONSE_TABLE;
```

The above code fragment declares the class TMyWindow as a descendant of the OWL class TWindow. The class declaration contains the member functions EvLButtonDown(), EvMove(), and EvPaint(). These functions handle messages generated by clicking the left mouse button (the Windows message WM_LBUTTONDOWN), moving the window (the Windows message WM_MOVE), and repainting the window (the Windows message WM_PAINT). The class declaration includes the macro DECLARE_RESPONSE_TABLE(TMyWindow). The DECLARE_RESPONSE_TABLE macro requires a single argument, the name of the class being declared. This macro instructs the compiler to build a vacant message-mapping table.

The code fragment includes the DEFINE_RESPONSE_TABLE1 macro that defines the message-response map. The 1 at the end of the macro name specifies that the declared class (TMyWindow) is the descendant of a single parent class. The macro includes the arguments of the declared class and its parent classes. If you declare a class with three parent classes, you must utilize the macro DEFINE_RESPONSE_TABLE3. The message-mapping macro contains map entries that link the Windows messages with particular event-handling member functions.

Borland C++ 4 supports two general types of map entries: predefined and user-defined. The *predefined* map entries have no arguments and map particular events to member functions with particular names. The above code fragment, for example, includes the predefined map entries EV_WM_LBUTTONDOWN, EV_WM_MOVE, and EV_WM_PAINT. The map entry EV_WM_LBUTTONDOWN maps the Windows message WM_LBUTTONDOWN with the member function EvLButtonDown(); the class TMyWindow declares this function. The map entry EV_WM_MOVE maps the Windows message WM_MOVE with the member function EvMove(); the class TMyWindow also declares this function. Similarly, the map entry EV_WM_PAINT maps the Windows message WM_PAINT with the member function EvPaint(), that also is declared in class TMyWindow.

The preceding message-map table also includes the EV_COMMAND map entry. EV_COMMAND is a user-defined entry that maps a Windows message command (CM_EXIT) with a member function (CmExit()).

The message-map table ends with the macro END_RESPONSE_TABLE. Each macro entry ends with a comma. The macro END_RESPONSE_TABLE ends with a semicolon. The Borland C++ manuals discuss the various kinds of message maps. Consult these manuals for more information.

The Minimal OWL Application

You begin any ObjectWindows application that you write by declaring a descendant of the OWL class TApplication. This mandatory step is required by even the most trivial ObjectWindows applications. The features of your application determine whether you can extend the other ObjectWindows classes. The other required component for an ObjectWindows application is the WinMain() function (similar to the main() function in a non-Windows C or C++ program) or the OwlMain() function. The ObjectWindows library includes the function WinMain() in the class TApplication.

The class TMyApp represents any application class that you derive from TApplication. The MyApp variable represents the application instance. The program creates this instance as a local variable in the special function OwlMain(). This function returns the result of sending the C++ message Run to the MyApp object.

The following code fragment is a template that gives you a general idea of the
basic makeup of your OWL-based programs. The code fragment shows that
in most cases you declare an application class and a main window class.

```
class TMyApp : public TApplication
{
public:
  // public data members declarations

  TMyApp() : TApplication() {}

// other constructors
// class destructors
// other member functions

protected:
  // protected data members
  virtual void InitMainWindow();
  virtual void InitInstance();      // optional
  virtual void InitApplication();   // optional
  virtual BOOL CanClose();          // optional
  // other protected member functions

private:
  // private data members
  // other private member functions
};

int OwlMain(int /* argc */, char** /* argv[] */)
{
    TMyApp app;
    return app.Run();
}
```

The preceding code fragment shows that your OWL-based application class
typically declares the member function InitMainWindow(). The declaration of
the member functions InitInstance(), InitApplication(), and CanClose() are
necessary only for fine-tuning the operations of these inherited functions in
your ObjectWindows application. This fact also applies to declaring constructor parameters, data members (public, protected, and private), and member
functions (public(), protected(), and private()).

Listing 14.1 shows the contents of the MINOWL.DEF definition file. Every
Windows application requires a definition file that specifies general param-
eters about the application. Listing 14.2 shows the source code for a minimal
OWL program that utilizes the preceding template. Notice that the
ObjectWindows application class TWinApp declares a constructor and the
InitMainWindow() member function. The InitMainWindow() function creates an

instance of TWindow, that is accessed by the inherited pointer-typed data member MainWindow. The instances of TWindow can be moved, resized, minimized, maximized, and it can have a Control menu. Figure 14.1 shows a sample session with the MINOWL.EXE application. To close the application window, use the **C**lose option in the system control menu or press the Alt+F4 keys.

When you create the MINOWL.IDE file to manage the minimal OWL program, include in that file the MINOWL.DEF and MINOWL.CPP files.

Figure 14.1.
A sample session with the MINOWL.EXE application.

Listing 14.1. The contents of the MINOWL.DEF definition file.

```
NAME          MinOwl
DESCRIPTION   'An OWL Windows Application'
EXETYPE       WINDOWS
CODE          PRELOAD MOVEABLE DISCARDABLE
DATA          PRELOAD MOVEABLE MULTIPLE
HEAPSIZE      1024
STACKSIZE     8192
```

Listing 14.2. The source code for the MINOWL.CPP program file.

```
/*
  Minimal OWL-based Windows program
*/
```

```
#include <owl\applicat.h>
#include <owl\framewin.h>

// declare the custom application class as
// a subclass of TApplication
class TMyApp : public TApplication
{
public:
  TMyApp() : TApplication() {}

protected:
  virtual void InitMainWindow();
};

void TMyApp::InitMainWindow()
{
  MainWindow = new TFrameWindow(0, "Minimal OWL-based Windows Program");
}

int OwlMain(int /* argc */, char** /*argv[] */)
{
  TMyApp app;
  return app.Run();
}
```

A Simple Interactive Windows Application

After having built a minimal ObjectWindows application, you are ready to write a new application that adds some functionality to the application's window. Listing 14.3 shows the contents of the CLICKAPP.DEF definition file. The source code for the CLICKAPP.CPP is presented in listing 14.4. Figure 14.2 shows a sample session with the CLICKAPP.EXE application. The program performs the following main tasks:

■ Responds to a left-button mouse click (when the mouse is inside the application window) by displaying a message box with an OK button.

■ Responds to a right-button mouse click by displaying a message box that asks you whether or not you want to close the window.

The application must declare a descendant of TWindow in order for the preceding tasks to implement the desired options.

Figure 14.2.
A sample session
with the
CLICKAPP.EXE
program.

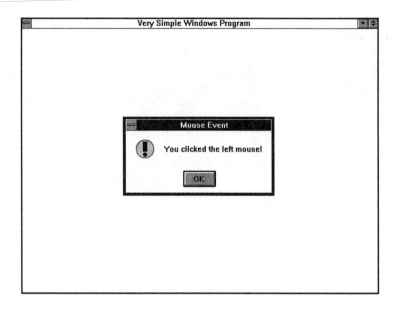

Listing 14.3. The contents of the CLICKAPP.DEF definition file.

```
NAME         ClickApp
DESCRIPTION  'An OWL Windows Application'
EXETYPE      WINDOWS
CODE         PRELOAD MOVEABLE DISCARDABLE
DATA         PRELOAD MOVEABLE MULTIPLE
HEAPSIZE     1024
STACKSIZE    8192
```

Listing 14.4. The source code for the CLICKAPP.CPP program file.

```
/*
  Program which responds to mouse button clicks
*/

#include <owl\applicat.h>
#include <owl\framewin.h>

// declare the custom application class as
// a subclass of TApplication
class TMyApp : public TApplication
{
public:
  TMyApp() : TApplication() {}

protected:
  virtual void InitMainWindow();
};
```

```
class TMyWindow : public TWindow
{
 public:
     TMyWindow() : TWindow(0, 0, 0) {}

 protected:

     // handle clicking the left mouse button
     void EvLButtonDown(UINT, TPoint&);

     // handle clicking the right mouse button
     void EvRButtonDown(UINT, TPoint&);

     // handle confirming closing the window
     virtual BOOL CanClose();

     // declare the response table
     DECLARE_RESPONSE_TABLE(TMyWindow);

};

DEFINE_RESPONSE_TABLE1(TMyWindow, TWindow)
  EV_WM_LBUTTONDOWN,
  EV_WM_RBUTTONDOWN,
END_RESPONSE_TABLE;

void TMyWindow::EvLButtonDown(UINT, TPoint&)
{
  MessageBox("You clicked the left mouse!", "Mouse Event",
            MB_OK | MB_ICONEXCLAMATION);
}

void TMyWindow::EvRButtonDown(UINT, TPoint&)
{
  Parent->SendMessage(WM_CLOSE);
}

BOOL TMyWindow::CanClose()
{
  return MessageBox("Want to close this application?",
                "Query", MB_YESNO | MB_ICONQUESTION) == IDYES;
}

void TMyApp::InitMainWindow()
{
  MainWindow = new TFrameWindow(0, "Very Simple Windows Program",
                    new TMyWindow);
}

int OwlMain(int /* argc */, char** /*argv[] */)
{
  TMyApp app;
  return app.Run();
}
```

Listing 14.4 shows the declaration of the TMyWindow class, a descendant of TWindow. The new class declares a constructor and two message-response member functions. The TMyWindow constructor simply calls the TWindow constructor, because no additional class instantiation is needed. The member functions EvLButtonDown() and EvRButtonDown() respond to the WM_LBUTTONDOWN and WM_RBUTTONDOWN messages, respectively. The message-response table indicates the default association between these member functions and messages, as shown in the following code:

```
DEFINE_RESPONSE_TABLE1(TMyWindow, TWindow)
  EV_WM_LBUTTONDOWN,
  EV_WM_RBUTTONDOWN,
END_RESPONSE_TABLE;
```

The table entry EV_WM_LBUTTONDOWN tells the compiler to use the member function EvLButtonDown() to handle the Windows message WM_LBUTTONDOWN. Similarly, the table entry EV_WM_RBUTTONDOWN tells the compiler to use the member function EvRButtonDown() to handle the Windows message WM_RBUTTONDOWN. The above table entries rely on using the specific member function names EvLButtonDown() and EvRButtonDown().

The EvLButtonDown() member function simply calls the function MessageBox() to display the string You clicked the left button! in a Mouse Event message box (refer to fig. 14.2). To resume program execution, you click the OK button in the message box.

The code for the EvRButtonDown sends the WM_CLOSE Windows message to the parent window. The function performs this task by sending the C++ message (not a Windows message) SendMessage to the object accessed by the pointer Parent. The argument of the SendMessage message is WM_CLOSE.

The Boolean member function CanClose() serves to check whether the window can be closed. If CLICKAPP.CPP implements a text editor, for example, you must make sure that you save updated or new text. The function calls the function MessageBox() to display a Query dialog box with the message Want to close this application?, Yes and No buttons, and a question-mark icon. The function compares the value of function MessageBox() with the predefined constant IDYES, then returns the Boolean result generated by the comparison.

The application class is very similar to the class in file MINOWL.CPP. The difference between the two classes is that the InitMainWindow() member function creates a new instance of TMyWindow, instead of TWindow.

The CALC Calculator Application

This section examines an application that uses single-line and multiline edit controls. The CALC application implements a floating-point calculator that uses edit controls instead of buttons. Figure 14.3 shows a sample session with the CALC program. In some ways, this kind of user interface is visually inferior to the typical multiple-button calculator Windows applications. Nevertheless, the interface presented here can support additional mathematical functions and does not require more buttons for these extra functions. The calculator has the following controls:

- The Operand1 and Operand2 edit controls for the first and second operands. These controls accept integers, floating point numbers, and the names of single-letter variables, A to Z.

- The Operator edit control for the operator. The present version of the calculator supports the four basic math operations and the exponentiation (using the ^ character).

- The Result edit control that displays the result of the math operation.

- The Error Message edit control that displays any error messages.

- The Variables multiline edit control that enables you to store a number in the Result edit control in one of 26 single-letter variables (A to Z). The multiline edit control displays the current values stored in these variables and enables you to view and edit these numbers. You can use the vertical scroll bar to inspect the values in the different variables.

- Multiple static text controls that serve to label the various edit controls. The static control for the Error Message box is of particular interest. If you click on the accompanying static text, the Error Message is cleared of any text.

- A menu with a single option, E**x**it.

- The **C**alc button that causes the program to execute the operation you specify in the Operand edit control. To cause this execution, the program uses the operands in the edit controls Operand1 and Operand2. You also can press Alt+C to invoke this button.

- The **S**tore button that causes the program to store the number of the Result edit control in the currently selected line of the Variables edit control. You can press the Alt+S keys to invoke this control. When you save a value in a variable, the program automatically chooses the next variable.

- The **E**xit button that enables you to exit the application.

The calculator application supports the following special features:

- The Error Message edit control clears its text if you click the left mouse button while the mouse cursor is positioned over the label `Error Message`.

- The **S**tore button is disabled if the application attempts to execute an invalid operator. This feature illustrates an example of disabling a command button when a certain condition arises (in this case, a specific calculation error).

- The **S**tore button is enabled if you click on the Error Message static text. The same button is enabled when you successfully execute a math operation.

The calculator application demonstrates the following program aspects:

- Using single-line edit controls for simple input.

- Using a multiline edit control to view and edit information.

- The line-oriented text access and editing.

- The simulation of static text that responds to mouse clicks.

- Using pushbuttons.

- Enabling and disabling pushbuttons.

- Associating accelerator keys with pushbuttons. This feature enables the program to maintain the same hot keys used by the menu items of the previous version.

You can get a good feel for how the calculator application works by compiling and running the application. Experiment with typing different numeric operands and the supported operators and click the **C**alc pushbutton. Each time you perform this operation, the result overwrites the previous result in the Result box. Try dividing a number by zero to experiment with the error-handling features.

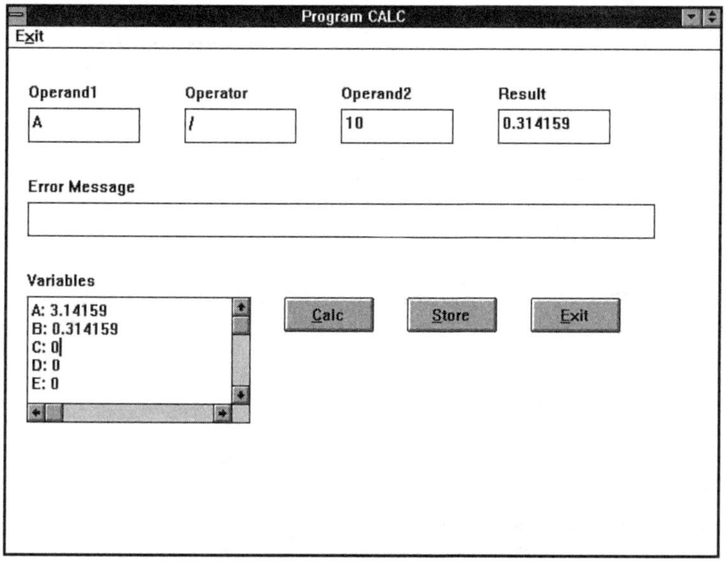

Figure 14.3.
A sample session with the CALC.EXE program.

Using the single-letter variables is a very easy operation. The program initializes these variables with 0. To use these variables, therefore, your first step is to store in them a non-zero value. Perform an operation and then click inside the Variables edit box. Click the **S**tore button (or press the Alt+S keys) and observe that the number in the Result box appears in the first line of the Variables edit box. The name of the variable (and the colon and space characters that follow) reappear with the new text line. Now replace the contents of the Operand1 edit box with the variable A, then click the **C**alc button. The Result edit box displays the result of the latest operation.

When you store a number in a variable, the insertion point moves on to the next line. Consequently, you can store the same result in neighboring variables by repeatedly pressing Alt+S.

Listing 14.5 shows the contents of the CALC.DEF definition file, and listing 14.6 contains the source code for the CALC.H header file. The file contains the various CM_XXXX and IDC_XXXX constants used by the calculator application. Listing 14.7 contains the script for the CALC.RC resource file. The resource file reveals a single item menu resource. In addition, the resource file also declares the accelerator keys resources. These accelerator keys associate the Alt+C, Alt+S, and Alt+E keys with their respective button IDs. Listing 14.8 shows the source code for the CALC.CPP program file.

Listing 14.5. The contents of the CALC.DEF definition file.

```
NAME          Calc
DESCRIPTION   'An OWL Windows Application'
EXETYPE       WINDOWS
CODE          PRELOAD MOVEABLE DISCARDABLE
DATA          PRELOAD MOVEABLE MULTIPLE
HEAPSIZE      1024
STACKSIZE     16384
```

Listing 14.6. The source code for the CALC.H header file.

```
#define IDC_CALC_BTN   100
#define IDC_STORE_BTN  101
#define IDC_EXIT_BTN   102
#define CM_CALC_BTN    103
#define CM_STORE_BTN   104
#define CM_EXIT_BTN    105
#define IDR_BUTTONS    200
#define IDM_EXITMENU   201
```

Listing 14.7. The script for the CALC.RC resource file.

```
#include <windows.h>
#include <owl\window.rh>
#include "calc.h"

IDR_BUTTONS ACCELERATORS
BEGIN
  "c", CM_CALC_BTN, ALT
  "s", CM_STORE_BTN, ALT
  "e", CM_EXIT_BTN, ALT
END

IDM_EXITMENU MENU LOADONCALL MOVEABLE PURE DISCARDABLE
BEGIN
    MENUITEM "E&xit", CM_EXIT
END
```

Listing 14.8. The source code for the CALC.CPP program file.

```
/*
  Program to test the static text, edit box, and push button controls.
  The program uses these controls to implement a command-line
  oriented calculator application
*/

#include <owl\applicat.h>
#include <owl\framewin.h>
#include <owl\static.h>
```

```
#include <owl\edit.h>
#include <owl\button.h>
#include <owl\window.rh>
#include "calc.h"
#include <stdlib.h>
#include <ctype.h>
#include <stdio.h>
#include <math.h>
#include <string.h>

// declare the constants that represent the sizes of the controls
const Wlbl = 100;
const Hlbl = 20;
const LblVertSpacing = 2;
const LblHorzSpacing = 40;
const Wbox = 100;
const Hbox = 30;
const BoxVertSpacing = 30;
const BoxHorzSpacing = 40;
const WLongbox = 4 * (Wbox + BoxHorzSpacing);
const Wvarbox = 2 * Wbox;
const Hvarbox = 3 * Hbox + 20;
const Hbtn = 30;
const Wbtn = 80;
const BtnHorzSpacing = 30;
const MaxEditLen = 30;
const MAX_MEMREG = 26;

// declare the IDC_XXXX constants for the edit boxes
#define IDC_OPERAND1_EDIT 101
#define IDC_OPERATOR_EDIT 102
#define IDC_OPERAND2_EDIT 103
#define IDC_RESULT_EDIT    104
#define IDC_ERRERRMSG_EDIT    105
#define IDC_VARIABLE_EDIT 106

// declare the custom application class as
// a subclass of TApplication
class TMyApp : public TApplication
{
public:
  TMyApp() : TApplication() {}

protected:
  virtual void InitMainWindow();
};

// expand the functionality of TWindow by
// deriving class TMyWindow
class TMyWindow : public TWindow
{
public:

  TMyWindow();
```

(continues)

Listing 14.8. Continued

```cpp
protected:

    // pointers to the controls
    TEdit* pOperand1Box;
    TEdit* pOperatorBox;
    TEdit* pOperand2Box;
    TEdit* pResultBox;
    TEdit* pErrMsgBox;
    TEdit* pVariableBox;
    TButton* pCalcBtn;
    TButton* pStoreBtn;
    TButton* pExitBtn;

    // math error flag
    BOOL InError;

    // coordinates for the Error Message static text area
    int ERRMSG_xulc, ERRMSG_yulc, ERRMSG_xlrc, ERRMSG_ylrc;

    //———————— member functions ————————

    // handle clicking the left mouse button
    void EvLButtonDown(UINT, TPoint&);

    // handle the accelerator key for the Calculate button
    void HandleCalcBtn();

    // handle the calculation
    void CMCalcBtn()
        { HandleCalcBtn(); }

    // handle the accelerator key for the Store button
    void HandleStoreBtn();

    // handle storing the result in a variable
    void CMStoreBtn()
        { HandleStoreBtn(); }

    // handle the accelerator key for the Exit button
    void HandleExitBtn();

    // handle exiting the application
    void CMExitBtn()
        { HandleExitBtn(); }

    // enable a push button control
    void EnableButton(TButton* pBtn)
        { pBtn->EnableWindow(TRUE); }

    // disable a push button control
    void DisableButton(TButton* pBtn)
        { pBtn->EnableWindow(FALSE); }
```

```
  // handle closing the window
  virtual BOOL CanClose();

  // obtain a number of a Variable edit box line
  double getVar(int lineNum);

  // store a number in the selected text of
  // the Variable edit box line
  void putVar(double x);

  // declare the message map macro
  DECLARE_RESPONSE_TABLE(TMyWindow);

};

DEFINE_RESPONSE_TABLE1(TMyWindow, TWindow)
  EV_WM_LBUTTONDOWN,
  EV_COMMAND(IDC_CALC_BTN, HandleCalcBtn),
  EV_COMMAND(CM_CALC_BTN, CMCalcBtn),
  EV_COMMAND(IDC_STORE_BTN, HandleStoreBtn),
  EV_COMMAND(CM_STORE_BTN, CMStoreBtn),
  EV_COMMAND(IDC_EXIT_BTN, HandleExitBtn),
  EV_COMMAND(CM_EXIT_BTN, CMExitBtn),
END_RESPONSE_TABLE;

TMyWindow::TMyWindow() :
           TWindow(0, 0, 0)
{
  char s[81];
  char bigStr[6 * MAX_MEMREG + 1];
  char c;
  int x0 = 20;
  int y0 = 30;
  int x = x0, y = y0;

  // create the first set of labels for the edit boxes
  strcpy(s, "Operand1");
  new TStatic(this, -1, s, x, y, Wlbl, Hlbl, strlen(s));
  strcpy(s, "Operator");
  x += Wlbl + LblHorzSpacing;
  new TStatic(this, -1, s, x, y, Wlbl, Hlbl, strlen(s));
  strcpy(s, "Operand2");
  x += Wlbl + LblHorzSpacing;
  new TStatic(this, -1, s, x, y, Wlbl, Hlbl, strlen(s));
  x += Wlbl + LblHorzSpacing;
  strcpy(s, "Result");
  new TStatic(this, -1, s, x, y, Wlbl, Hlbl, strlen(s));

  // create the operand1, operator, operand2, and result
  // edit boxes
  x = x0;
  y += Hlbl + LblVertSpacing;
  pOperand1Box = new TEdit(this, IDC_OPERAND1_EDIT, "", x, y,
                 Wbox, Hbox, 0, FALSE);
```

(continues)

Listing 14.8. Continued

```
// force conversion of letters to uppercase
pOperand1Box->Attr.Style |= ES_UPPERCASE;
x += Wbox + BoxHorzSpacing;
pOperatorBox = new TEdit(this, IDC_OPERATOR_EDIT, "", x, y,
                Wbox, Hbox, 0, FALSE);
x += Wbox + BoxHorzSpacing;
pOperand2Box = new TEdit(this, IDC_OPERAND2_EDIT, "", x, y,
                Wbox, Hbox, 0, FALSE);
// force conversion of letters to uppercase
pOperand2Box->Attr.Style |= ES_UPPERCASE;
x += Wbox + BoxHorzSpacing;
pResultBox = new TEdit(this, IDC_RESULT_EDIT, "", x, y, Wbox, Hbox,
                0, FALSE);

// create the static text and edit box for the error message
x = x0;
y += Hbox + BoxVertSpacing;
// store the coordinates for the static text area
ERRMSG_xulc = x;
ERRMSG_yulc = y;
ERRMSG_xlrc = x + Wlbl;
ERRMSG_ylrc = y + Hlbl;
strcpy(s, "Error Message");
new TStatic(this, -1, s, x, y, Wlbl, Hlbl, strlen(s));
y += Hlbl + LblVertSpacing;
pErrMsgBox = new TEdit(this, IDC_ERRERRMSG_EDIT, "", x, y,
             WLongbox, Hbox, 0, FALSE);
// create the static text and edit box for the single-letter
// variable selection
y += Hbox + BoxVertSpacing;
strcpy(s, "Variables");
new TStatic(this, -1, s, x, y, Wlbl, Hlbl, strlen(s));
y += Hlbl + LblVertSpacing;
bigStr[0] = '\0';
// build the initial contents of the Variable edit box
for (c = 'A'; c <= 'Z'; c++) {
  sprintf(s, "%c: 0\r\n", c);
  strcat(bigStr, s);
}
pVariableBox = new TEdit(this, IDC_VARIABLE_EDIT, bigStr, x, y,
                Wvarbox, Hvarbox, 0, TRUE);
// force conversion of letters to uppercase
pVariableBox->Attr.Style |= ES_UPPERCASE;

// create the Calc push button
x += Wvarbox + BtnHorzSpacing;
pCalcBtn = new TButton(this, IDC_CALC_BTN, "&Calc",
             x, y, Wbtn, Hbtn, FALSE);

// create the Store Btn
x += Wbtn + BtnHorzSpacing;
pStoreBtn = new TButton(this, IDC_STORE_BTN, "&Store",
                x, y, Wbtn, Hbtn, FALSE);
```

```
    // Create the Exit Btn
    x += Wbtn + BtnHorzSpacing;
    pExitBtn = new TButton(this, IDC_EXIT_BTN, "&Exit",
                    x, y, Wbtn, Hbtn, FALSE);

    // clear the InError flag
    InError = FALSE;

    UpdateWindow();
}

void TMyWindow::EvLButtonDown(UINT, TPoint& point)
{
    if (point.x >= ERRMSG_xulc && point.x <= ERRMSG_xlrc &&
            point.y >= ERRMSG_yulc && point.y <= ERRMSG_ylrc) {
        pErrMsgBox->Clear();
        // enable the Store button
        EnableButton(pStoreBtn);
    }
}

void TMyWindow::HandleCalcBtn()
{
    double x, y, z;
    char opStr[MaxEditLen+1];
    char s[MaxEditLen+1];

    // obtain the string in the Operand1 edit box
    pOperand1Box->GetText(s, MaxEditLen);
    // does the Operand1Box contain the name
    // of a single-letter variable?
    if (isalpha(s[0]))
      // obtain value from the Variable edit control
        x = getVar(s[0] - 'A');
    else
      // convert the string in the edit box
      x = atof(s);

    // obtain the string in the Operand2 edit box
    pOperand2Box->GetText(s, MaxEditLen);
    // does the pOperand2Box contain the name
    // of a single-letter variable?
    if (isalpha(s[0]))
      // obtain value from the Variable edit control
        y = getVar(s[0] - 'A');
    else
        // convert the string in the edit box
      y = atof(s);

    // obtain the string in the Operator edit box
    pOperatorBox->GetText(opStr, MaxEditLen);

    // clear the error message box
    pErrMsgBox->Clear();
    InError = FALSE;
```

(continues)

Listing 14.8. Continued

```
// determine the requested operation
if (strcmp(opStr, "+") == 0)
  z = x + y;
else if (strcmp(opStr, "-") == 0)
  z = x - y;
else if (strcmp(opStr, "*") == 0)
  z = x * y;
else if (strcmp(opStr, "/") == 0) {
  if (y != 0)
        z = x / y;
  else {
    z = 0;
    InError = TRUE;
    pErrMsgBox->SetText("Division-by-zero error");
  }
}
else if (strcmp(opStr, "^") == 0) {
  if (x > 0)
    z = exp(y * log(x));
  else {
    InError = TRUE;
        pErrMsgBox->SetText(
    "Cannot raise the power of a negative number");
  }
}
else {
  InError = TRUE;
    pErrMsgBox->SetText("Invalid operator");
}
// display the result if no error has occurred
if (!InError) {
  sprintf(s, "%g", z);
  pResultBox->SetText(s);
  // enable the Store button
  EnableButton(pStoreBtn);
}
else
  // disable the Store button
    DisableButton(pStoreBtn);
}

void TMyWindow::HandleStoreBtn()
{
  char result[MaxEditLen+1];

  // get the string in the Result edit box
  pResultBox->GetText(result, MaxEditLen);

  // store the result in the selected text of
  // the Variable edit box
  putVar(atof(result));
}
```

```
void TMyWindow::HandleExitBtn()
{
  // send a WM_CLOSE message to the parent window
  Parent->SendMessage(WM_CLOSE);
}

double TMyWindow::getVar(int lineNum)
{
  int lineSize;
  char s[MaxEditLen+1];

  if (lineNum >= MAX_MEMREG) return 0;
  // get the size of the target line
  lineSize = pVariableBox->GetLineLength(lineNum);
  // get the line
  pVariableBox->GetLine(s, lineSize+1, lineNum);
  // delete the first three characters
  strcpy(s, (s+3));
  // return the number stored in the target line
  return atof(s);
}

void TMyWindow::putVar(double x)
{
  UINT startPos, endPos;
  int lineNum;
  int lineSize;
  char s[MaxEditLen+1];

  // locate the character position of the cursor
  pVariableBox->GetSelection(startPos, endPos);
  // turn off the selected text
  if (startPos != endPos)
    pVariableBox->SetSelection(startPos, startPos);
  // get the line number where the cursor is located
  lineNum = pVariableBox->GetLineFromPos(startPos);
  // get the line size of line lineNum
  lineSize = pVariableBox->GetLineLength(lineNum);
  // obtain the text of line lineNum
  pVariableBox->GetLine(s, lineSize+1, lineNum);
  // delete line lineNum
  pVariableBox->DeleteLine(lineNum);
  // build the new text line
  sprintf(s, "%c: %g\r\n", s[0], x);
  // insert it
  pVariableBox->Insert(s);
}

BOOL TMyWindow::CanClose()
{
  return MessageBox("Close this application?",
                "Query", MB_YESNO | MB_ICONQUESTION) == IDYES;
}
```

(continues)

Listing 14.8. Continued

```
void TMyApp::InitMainWindow()
{
  MainWindow = new TFrameWindow(0, "Program CALC", new TMyWindow);
  // load the keystroke resources
  MainWindow->Attr.AccelTable = IDR_BUTTONS;
  // load the menu resource
  MainWindow->AssignMenu(TResID(IDM_EXITMENU));
  // enable the keyboard handler
  MainWindow->EnableKBHandler();
}

int OwlMain(int /* argc */, char** /*argv[] */)
{
  TMyApp app;
  return app.Run();
}
```

The CALC program declares a set of constants, the application class, TMyApp, and the main window class, TMyWindow. The set of constants includes one for the control locations, sizes and dimensions. The TMyWindow window class is the owner of the static text and edit controls. The class declares a number of data members and member functions.

The class TMyWindow contains the following groups of data members:

- Pointers to the various TEdit instances. Each pointer accesses one of the edit controls that appear in the program.

- Pointers to the various TButton instances. Each pointer accesses one of the command button controls that appear in the program.

- The Boolean data member InError flags any error.

- The ERRMSG_XXXX data members that store the coordinates for the rectangle that contains the Error Message static text. The mouse-click response member function EvLButtonDown() examines whether or not the mouse is clicked inside that rectangle. If so, the member function clears the Error Message edit control text.

The TMyWindow class contains a constructor and a number of message response member functions that handle the mouse-click and respond to the menu options.

The window class constructor performs the following tasks:

- Creates the static text controls that label the Operand1, Operator, Oper-and1, and Result edit controls by invoking the TStatic constructor. The local variable x is increased by (Wlbl + LblHorzSpacing) to calculate the X coordinate for the next static text control. This approach is easier than plugging in numbers in the TStatic constructor.

- Creates the edit boxes for the operands, operator, and the result. The instances for these controls are accessed by the Operand1Box, OperatorBox, Operand2Box, and ResultBox data members. Each TEdit instance is created with its own IDC_XXXX constant, and an empty edit box. The edit boxes are the same size. The constructor modifies the style of the operand edit controls to include the ES_UPPERCASE style (to convert the single-letter variable names that you type in these edit controls into uppercase). The argument for the parameter text in the single-line controls is 0, to indicate that there is no limit on the amount of text to store. The argument for the parameter multiLine is FALSE, to indicate that these controls are single-line edit boxes.

- Calculates the upper-left corner and lower-right corner of the rectangle containing the Error Message text and stores them in the ERRMSG_XXXX data members.

- Creates the error message static text control and edit control.

- Creates the Variables multiline edit control. This task begins by building the contents of the Variables box using the string variable bigStr. The TEdit constructor uses the bigStr variable as the initial text for the control. The argument for the parameter text is 0, to indicate that there is no limit on the amount of text to store. The argument for the parameter multiLine is TRUE to indicate that the control is a multiline edit box. The style of the Variables edit control also is set to force the conversion of letters into uppercase.

- Creates the command button instances, using the following statements:

```
pCalcBtn = new TButton(this, IDC_CALC_BTN, "&Calc",
                       x, y, Wbtn, Hbtn, FALSE);

pStoreBtn = new TButton(this, IDC_STORE_BTN, "&Store",
                        x, y, Wbtn, Hbtn, FALSE);
```

```
pExitBtn = new TButton(this, IDC_EXIT_BTN, "&Exit",
                       x, y, Wbtn, Hbtn, FALSE);
```

■ The constructor creates each TButton instance with a unique ID and caption. The caption uses the ampersand character to underline the hot key. The last argument in all of the above three statements supplies FALSE to the parameter isDefault. Although these argument values explicitly specify that neither button is the default button, they are irrelevant, because the buttons are created in a non-dialog window. You can use a TRUE value in either constructor and still wind up with the same result.

■ Sets the InError data member to FALSE.

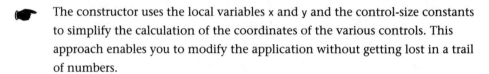 The constructor uses the local variables x and y and the control-size constants to simplify the calculation of the coordinates of the various controls. This approach enables you to modify the application without getting lost in a trail of numbers.

The program uses the response-table macro to map the various events and commands onto their respective handlers. The program uses the macro EV_WM_LBUTTONDOWN and the member function EvLButtonDown() to handle the left mouse-button click. The other map entries are the EV_COMMAND macros that relate the various CM_XXXX_BTN and IDC_XXXX_BTN commands to their corresponding CMXXXXBtn() and HandleXXXXBtn() member functions.

The member functions EnableButton() and DisableButton() enable and disable a command button by calling the EnableWindow() function. These functions are called by other member functions that pass the argument StoreBtn to enable or disable the Store pushbutton.

The member function EvLButtonDown() performs a simple task. It checks whether or not the mouse-click occurs in the rectangle occupied by the error message static text control. If this condition is true, the function clears the error message box by invoking the Clear() function. In addition, the function enables the **S**tore button.

The member function HandleCalcBtn() responds to a click of the **C**alc pushbutton and performs the calculation using the operands and operators that appear in their respective edit controls. The function HandleCalcBtn() performs the following tasks:

■ Obtains the first operand from the Operand1 edit box. The control may contain the name of a single-letter variable (A to Z) or a floating point number. The function uses the GetText() function to store a copy of the edit control text in the local variable s. The function then examines the first character in variable s. If that character is a letter, then the first operand is a single-letter variable. Consequently, the function calls the protected member function getVar() to obtain the value associated with that variable. If the first character is not a letter, the function uses the atof() function to convert the contents of variable s into a double-typed number. In both cases, the function stores the actual (numeric) first operand in variable x.

■ Obtains the second operand in a manner identical to the way it obtained the first one. The function stores the actual (numeric) second operand in variable y.

■ Copies the text in the Operator edit box into the local variable opStr.

■ Clears the error message text box and sets the InError data member to FALSE.

■ Determines the requested operation by using a series of if and if-else statements. The operators supported are +, -, *, /, and ^ (power.) If the function detects an error, it assigns TRUE to the data member InError and displays a message in the error message box.

■ Displays the result in the Result box if the InError data member is FALSE. The function first converts the result from double to a string and then writes to the Result box using the SetText() function. If the member InError is TRUE, the function disables the **S**tore button by using the member function DisableButton().

The member function CMCalcBtn() responds to the CM_CALC_BTN command generated by pressing the Alt+C keys. The function merely calls the member function HandleCalcBtn().

The member function HandleStoreBtn() responds to the command IDC_STORE_BTN by storing the contents of the Result box in a single-letter variable. The function first obtains the string in the Result edit box by calling the GetText() function. Then, the function invokes the protected member function putVar() to actually store the result string at the current insertion point in the Variables edit box.

The member function CMStoreBtn() responds to the CM_STORE_BTN command generated by pressing the Alt+S keys. The function merely calls the member function HandleStoreBtn().

 The member functions HandleExitBtn() and CMExitBtn() close the window by sending the Windows message WM_CLOSE to the parent window. The application uses an instance of TMyWindow as a client window in an instance of TFrameWindow (this operation is explained later in this chapter).

The member function getVar() returns the number stored at line number lineNum of the Variables edit box. The function performs the following tasks:

- Exits and returns 0 if the lineNum is greater than or equal to the constant MAX_MEMREG.

- Obtains the size of the target line by making the GetLineLength(lineNum) call.

- Retrieves the strings of line number lineNum by calling the GetLine() function.

- Deletes the first three characters of the retrieved line. This step should leave the string with the number stored in the target line.

- Returns the double-typed number obtained by calling the atof() function and supplying it argument s.

The member function putVar() stores the number in the Result box in the variable that is located on the same line that contains the text insert position. The function performs the following tasks:

- Locates the character position of the cursor by calling the GetSelection() function. The function returns the start and end character positions in the local variables startPos and endPos.

- Turns off any selected text. The function compares the values in the variables startPos and endPos. If these values do not match, the function invokes the SetSelection() function and supplies it with the startPos as both the first and second arguments. This invocation of SetSelection() turns off the selected text.

- Obtains the line number where the cursor is located using the GetLineFromPos() function.

- Obtains the size of the target line using the `GetLineLength()` function.

- Retrieves the text in the target line by calling the `GetLine()` function.

- Deletes the target line using the `DeleteLine()` function.

- Builds the string for the new line.

- Inserts the new line by calling the `Insert()` function.

The application class `TMyApp` declares the member function `InitMainWindow()`. This member function performs the following tasks:

- Creates the main window as an instance of `TFrameWindow`. This task also specifies the window's title and uses an instance of class `TMyWindow` as the client window. The function assigns the address of the `TFrameWindow` instance to the inherited data member `MainWindow`.

- Loads the keystroke resources identifier by the ID `IDR_BUTTONS`.

- Loads the menu resource `IDM_EXITMENU`. This task sends the message `AssignMenu` to the main window component of the application.

- Enables the keyboard handler by sending the message `EnableKBHandler` to the main window part of the application.

The Text Editor Application

The following portion of this chapter gives you a glimpse of the power and versatility of the AppExpert utility. This utility generates skeleton code for OWL-based programs. Typically, such programs are minimally functional and require additional customization to support specific features. You can invoke this application-generating utility from the **P**roject menu selection. The AppExpert first brings up a file selection dialog box in which you can specify the target directory for the project you want to create. You also can select a new or existing IDE file. If you select an existing IDE file, the AppExpert utility adds the new application to that IDE file. Select the appropriate target directory and enter the IDE file name EDITOR.IDE. Click the OK button. The AppExpert utility then brings up the AppExpert dialog box, shown in figure 14.4. The dialog box has three main sets of options, labeled Application, Main Window, and MDI Child/View. You can inspect the options offered for each aspect of the application. Click the **G**enerate button to generate the source code files for the editor. The AppExpert utility requests that you confirm your request to generate the source code for the text editor project. After you give your confirmation, the AppExpert utility begins to generate the files for the EDITOR.IDE project.

Figure 14.4.
The AppExpert
Application
Generation
Options dialog
box.

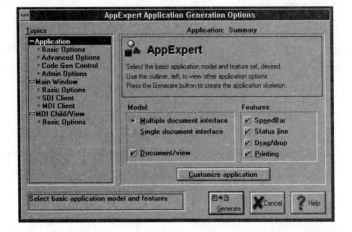

Press the Ctrl+F9 keys to build and run the EDITOR.EXE file. The Borland C++ IDE produces a minimal text editor application. Figure 14.5 shows a sample session with the EDITOR.EXE program. This application supports MDI (*Multiple Document Interface*) windows and has a speed bar and a status bar. Further, the program has a non-trivial menu system with editing and printing options. You can open text files and edit their text by using the cut, copy, and paste operations. You also can use the find and replace menu items to edit the contents of text file. The printing feature is somewhat disappointing, because the program prints your text files as tiny graphics images! Well, nothing is perfect in life.

The power of the AppExpert utility is in its capability to generate a sophisticated (albeit, imperfect) program without requiring that you write a single line of code. The AppExpert emits a whole set of header, resource, definition, and source code files. An in-depth discussion of these files is beyond the scope of this book. However, the following listings offer you a small taste of the files generated by the AppExpert utility. Listing 14.9 shows the contents of the EDITRAPP.DEF definition file. Listing 14.10 shows the source code of the EDITRAPP.H header file. Listing 14.11 contains the source code for the EDITRAPP.CPP implementation file.

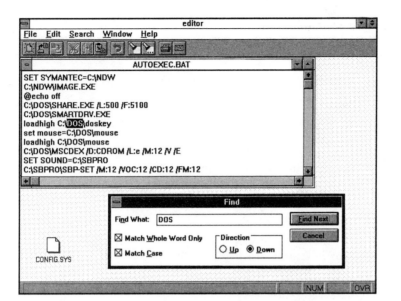

Figure 14.5.
A sample session
with the
EDITOR.EXE
program.

Listing 14.9. The contents of the EDITRAPP.DEF definition file.

```
;  — — — — — — — — — — — — — — — — — — — — — — — —
;    Main editor
;
;    Copyright © 1993. All Rights Reserved.
;
;    SUBSYSTEM:     editor.exe Module Definition File
;    FILE:          editrapp.def
;    AUTHOR:
;
;  — — — — — — — — — — — — — — — — — — — — — — — —

NAME editor

DESCRIPTION 'editor Application - Copyright © 1993 All Rights Reserved. '
EXETYPE      WINDOWS
CODE         PRELOAD MOVEABLE DISCARDABLE
DATA         PRELOAD MOVEABLE MULTIPLE
HEAPSIZE     4096
STACKSIZE    8192
```

Listing 14.10. The source code for the EDITRAPP.H header file.

```
#if !defined(__editrapp_h)     // Sentry, use file only if it's

                               // not already included.
#define __editrapp_h

/*  Project editor
```
(continues)

Listing 14.10. Continued

```
        Copyright © 1993. All Rights Reserved.

        SUBSYSTEM:    editor.exe Application
        FILE:         editrapp.h
        AUTHOR:


        OVERVIEW
        ========
        Class definition for editorApp (TApplication).
*/


#include <owl\owlpch.h>
#pragma hdrstop

#include <owl\statusba.h>
#include <owl\controlb.h>
#include <owl\buttonga.h>
#include <owl\editview.h>
#include <owl\listview.h>
#include <owl\docmanag.h>
#include <owl\filedoc.h>
#include <owl\printer.h>

#include <classlib\bags.h>


#include "editrapp.rh"          // Definition of all resources.


// TFileDrop class Maintains information about a dropped file, its
// name, where it was dropped, and whether or not it was in the
// client area
class TFileDrop {
public:
    operator == (const TFileDrop& other) const {return this == &other;}

    char*   FileName;
    TPoint  Point;
    BOOL    InClientArea;

    HICON   Icon;
    BOOL    DefIcon;

    TFileDrop (char*, TPoint&, BOOL, TModule* module);
    ~TFileDrop ();

    const char* WhoAmI ();
private:
    //
```

```
        // hidden to prevent accidental copying or assignment
        //
        TFileDrop (const TFileDrop&);
        TFileDrop & operator = (const TFileDrop&);
    };

    typedef TIBagAsVector<TFileDrop> TFileList;
    typedef TIBagAsVectorIterator<TFileDrop> TFileListIter;


    //{{TApplication = editorApp}}
    class editorApp : public TApplication {
    private:

    private:
        void SetupSpeedBar (TDecoratedMDIFrame *frame);
        void AddFiles (TFileList* files);

    public:
        editorApp ();
        virtual ~editorApp ();

        // Public data members used by the print menu commands and
        // Paint routine in MDIChild.
        TPrinter      *Printer;           // Printer support.
        BOOL          Printing;           // Printing in progress.

    //{{editorAppVIRTUAL_BEGIN}}
    public:
        virtual void InitMainWindow();
        virtual void InitInstance();
    //{{editorAppVIRTUAL_END}}

    //{{editorAppRSP_TBL_BEGIN}}
    protected:
        void EvNewView (TView& view);
        void EvCloseView (TView& view);
        void CmHelpAbout ();
        void EvDropFiles (TDropInfo drop);
        void EvWinIniChange (char far* section);
    //{{editorAppRSP_TBL_END}}
      DECLARE_RESPONSE_TABLE(editorApp);
    };    //{{editorApp}}


    #endif                               // __editrapp_h sentry.
```

Listing 14.11. The source code for the EDITRAPP.CPP program file.

```
/*  Project editor

    Copyright © 1993. All Rights Reserved.
```

(continues)

Listing 14.11. Continued

```
      SUBSYSTEM:     editor.exe Application
      FILE:          editrapp.cpp
      AUTHOR:


      OVERVIEW
      ========
      Source file for implementation of editorApp (TApplication).
*/


#include <owl\owlpch.h>
#pragma hdrstop

#include <dir.h>

#include "editrapp.h"
#include "dtrmdicl.h"
#include "dtrmdich.h"
#include "dtrabtdl.h"                  // Definition of about dialog.


// Drag / Drop support:
TFileDrop::TFileDrop (char* fileName, TPoint& p, BOOL inClient,
                      TModule* module)
{
    char    exePath[MAXPATH];

    exePath[0] = 0;
    FileName = strcpy(new char[strlen(fileName) + 1], fileName);
    Point = p;
    InClientArea = inClient;

    Icon = (WORD)FindExecutable(FileName, ".\\", exePath) <= 32 ?
                  0 : ::ExtractIcon(*module, exePath, 0);

    // Use a question mark if couldn't get the icon from the

    // executable.
    if ((WORD)Icon <= 1) {  // 0=no icons in exe,  1=not an exe
        Icon = LoadIcon(0, (WORD)Icon == 1 ?
                    IDI_APPLICATION : IDI_QUESTION);
        DefIcon = TRUE;
    } else
        DefIcon = FALSE;
}

TFileDrop::~TFileDrop ()
{
    delete FileName;
```

```
        if (!DefIcon)
            FreeResource(Icon);
}

const char *TFileDrop::WhoAmI ()
{
  return FileName;
}


//{{editorApp Implementation}}

//{{DOC_VIEW}}
DEFINE_DOC_TEMPLATE_CLASS(TFileDocument, TEditView, DocType1);
//{{DOC_VIEW_END}}

//{{DOC_MANAGER}}
DocType1 __dvt1("All Files (*.*)", "*.*", 0, "TXT",
                dtAutoDelete | dtUpdateDir);
//{{DOC_MANAGER_END}}

//
// Build a response table for all messages/commands handled
// by the application.
//
DEFINE_RESPONSE_TABLE1(editorApp, TApplication)
//{{editorAppRSP_TBL_BEGIN}}
    EV_OWLVIEW(dnCreate, EvNewView),
    EV_OWLVIEW(dnClose,  EvCloseView),
    EV_COMMAND(CM_HELPABOUT, CmHelpAbout),
    EV_WM_DROPFILES,
    EV_WM_WININICHANGE,
//{{editorAppRSP_TBL_END}}
END_RESPONSE_TABLE;


///////////////////////////////////////////////////////
// editorApp
// =====
//
editorApp::editorApp () : TApplication("editor")
{

    Printer = 0;
    Printing = FALSE;

    DocManager = new TDocManager(dmMDI | dmMenu);

    // INSERT>> Your constructor code here.

}


editorApp::~editorApp ()
{
    if (Printer)
```

(continues)

Listing 14.11. Continued

```
            delete Printer;

        // INSERT>> Your destructor code here.

    }


    void editorApp::SetupSpeedBar (TDecoratedMDIFrame *frame)
    {
        //
        // Create default toolbar New and associate toolbar buttons
        // with commands.
        //
        TControlBar* cb = new TControlBar(frame);
        cb->Insert(*new TButtonGadget(CM_MDIFILENEW, CM_MDIFILENEW));
        cb->Insert(*new TButtonGadget(CM_MDIFILEOPEN, CM_MDIFILEOPEN));
        cb->Insert(*new TButtonGadget(CM_FILESAVE, CM_FILESAVE));
        cb->Insert(*new TSeparatorGadget(6));
        cb->Insert(*new TButtonGadget(CM_EDITCUT, CM_EDITCUT));
        cb->Insert(*new TButtonGadget(CM_EDITCOPY, CM_EDITCOPY));
        cb->Insert(*new TButtonGadget(CM_EDITPASTE, CM_EDITPASTE));
        cb->Insert(*new TSeparatorGadget(6));
        cb->Insert(*new TButtonGadget(CM_EDITUNDO, CM_EDITUNDO));
        cb->Insert(*new TSeparatorGadget(6));
        cb->Insert(*new TButtonGadget(CM_EDITFIND, CM_EDITFIND));
        cb->Insert(*new TButtonGadget(CM_EDITFINDNEXT, CM_EDITFINDNEXT));
        cb->Insert(*new TSeparatorGadget(6));
        cb->Insert(*new TButtonGadget(CM_FILEPRINT, CM_FILEPRINT));
        cb->Insert(*new TButtonGadget(CM_FILEPRINTPREVIEW,
                                      CM_FILEPRINTPREVIEW));

        // Add fly-over help hints.
        cb->SetHintMode(TGadgetWindow::EnterHints);

        frame->Insert(*cb, TDecoratedFrame::Top);
    }


    //////////////////////////////////////////////////////////
    // editorApp
    // =====
    // Application intialization.
    //
    void editorApp::InitMainWindow ()
    {
        TDecoratedMDIFrame* frame = new TDecoratedMDIFrame(Name, MDI_MENU,
                    *(new editorMDIClient), TRUE);

        nCmdShow = (nCmdShow != SW_SHOWMINNOACTIVE) ?
                        SW_SHOWNORMAL : nCmdShow;
```

```
    //
    // Assign ICON w/ this application.
    //
    frame->SetIcon(this, IDI_MDIAPPLICATION);

    //
    //Menu associated with window and accelerator table associated

    // with table.
    //
    frame->AssignMenu(MDI_MENU);

    //
    // Associate with the accelerator table.
    //
    frame->Attr.AccelTable = MDI_MENU;


    SetupSpeedBar(frame);

    TStatusBar *sb = new TStatusBar(frame, TGadget::Recessed,
                                    TStatusBar::CapsLock        ¦
                                    TStatusBar::NumLock         ¦
                                    TStatusBar::ScrollLock      ¦
                                    TStatusBar::Overtype);
    frame->Insert(*sh, TDecoratedFrame::Bottom);

    MainWindow = frame;

}


///////////////////////////////////////////////////////
// editorApp
// =====
// Response Table handlers:
//
void editorApp::EvNewView (TView& view)
{
    TMDIClient *mdiClient = TYPESAFE_DOWNCAST(
        MainWindow->GetClientWindow(), TMDIClient);
    if (mdiClient) {
        editorMDIChild* child = new editorMDIChild(*mdiClient, 0,
                                        view.GetWindow());

        // Associate ICON w/ this child window.
        child->SetIcon(this, IDI_DOC);

        child->Create();
    }
}


void editorApp::EvCloseView (TView&)
{
}
```

(continues)

Listing 14.11. Continued

```
/////////////////////////////////////////////////////////
// editorApp
// ===========
// Menu Help About editor.exe command
void editorApp::CmHelpAbout ()
{
    //
    // Show the modal dialog.
    //
    editorAboutDlg(MainWindow).Execute();
}


void editorApp::InitInstance ()
{
    TApplication::InitInstance();

    // Accept files via drag/drop in the frame window.
    MainWindow->DragAcceptFiles(TRUE);
}


void editorApp::EvDropFiles (TDropInfo drop)
{
    // Number of files dropped.
    int totalNumberOfFiles = drop.DragQueryFileCount();

    TFileList* files = new TFileList;

    for (int i = 0; i < totalNumberOfFiles; i++) {
        // Tell DragQueryFile the file interested in (i) and the
        // length of your buffer.
        int     fileLength = drop.DragQueryFileNameLen(i) + 1;
        char    *fileName = new char[fileLength];

        drop.DragQueryFile(i, fileName, fileLength);

        // Getting the file dropped. The location is relative to
        // your client coordinates, and will have negative values
        // if dropped in the non-client parts of the window.
        //
        // DragQueryPoint copies that point where the file was
        // dropped and returns whether or not the point is in the
        // client area. Regardless of whether or not the file is
        // dropped in the client or non-client area of the window,
        // you will still receive the file name.
```

```
        TPoint  point;
        BOOL    inClientArea = drop.DragQueryPoint(point);
        files->Add(new TFileDrop(fileName, point, inClientArea, this));
    }

    // Open the files that were dropped.
    AddFiles(files);

    // Release the memory allocated for this handle with DragFinish.
    drop.DragFinish();
}


void editorApp::AddFiles (TFileList* files)
{
    // Open all files dragged in.
    TFileListIter fileIter(*files);

    while (fileIter) {
        TDocTemplate* tpl = GetDocManager()->MatchTemplate(
                        fileIter.Current()->WhoAmI());
        if (tpl)
            tpl->CreateDoc(fileIter.Current()->WhoAmI());
        fileIter++;
    }
}


void editorApp::EvWinIniChange (char far* section)
{
    if (lstrcmp(section, "windows") == 0) {
        // If the device changed in the WIN.INI file then the
        // printer might have changed.  If we have a TPrinter
        // (Printer) then check and make sure it's identical to the
        // current device entry in WIN.INI.
        if (Printer) {
            char printDBuffer[255];
            LPSTR printDevice = printDBuffer;
            LPSTR devName = 0;
            LPSTR driverName = 0;
            LPSTR outputName = 0;

            if (::GetProfileString("windows", "device", "", printDevice,
                            sizeof(printDevice))) {
                // The string which should come back is something
                // like:
                //      HP LaserJet III,hppcl5a,LPT1:
                //
                // Where the format is:
                //
```

(continues)

Listing 14.11. Continued

```
                                //      devName,driverName,outputName
                                //
                                devName = printDevice;
                                while (*printDevice) {
                                    if (*printDevice == ',') {
                                        *printDevice++ = 0;
                                        if (!driverName)
                                            driverName = printDevice;
                                        else
                                            outputName = printDevice;
                                    } else
                                        printDevice = AnsiNext(printDevice);
                                }

                                if ((Printer->GetSetup().Error != 0) ||
                                    (lstrcmp(devName,
                                    Printer->GetSetup().GetDeviceName()) != 0) ||
                                    (lstrcmp(driverName,
                                    Printer->GetSetup().GetDriverName()) != 0) ||
                                    (lstrcmp(outputName,
                                    Printer->GetSetup().GetOutputName()) != 0)) {

                                    // New printer installed so get the new printer
                                    // device now.
                                    delete Printer;
                                    Printer = new TPrinter;
                                }
                        } else {
                            // No printer installed (GetProfileString failed).
                            delete Printer;
                            Printer = new TPrinter;
                        }
                    }
                }
        }


int OwlMain (int , char* [])
{
    editorApp     App;
    int           result;

    result = App.Run();

    return result;
}
```

The definition file in listing 14.9 is very similar to the other DEF files presented earlier in this chapter.

The EDITRAPP.H header file in listing 14.10 declares the application class editorApp as a descendant of TApplication. The editor class also declares member functions to set up the speed bar and handle view-related events. The header file also contains the declaration of class TFileDrop. This class manages the data for the dropped file (as part of the drag-and-drop feature). This information includes the name of the dropped file, the drop location, and whether or not the drop location is in the client area.

The EDITRAPP.CPP implementation file in listing 14.11 defines the response table to handle the view-related events and then declares the following members:

1. The constructor has statements that initialize the members Printer and Printing and create the document manager. The constructor contains a comment-based placeholder where you can insert additional statements to support additional features.

2. The destructor deletes the dynamic printer object of the member Printer when that member is not a null pointer. The destructor also contains a comment-based placeholder where you can insert statements that deallocate dynamic memory and perform additional cleanup operations.

3. The member function SetupSpeedBar() creates the speed bar and associates its buttons with various menu commands.

4. The member function InitMainWindow() initializes the main window.

5. The member function EvNewView() handles creating a new view in the text editor.

6. The member function EvCloseView() is a skeleton to which you can add statements to perform additional cleanup operations when you close your customized views.

Listing 14.12 shows another header file generated by the AppExpert utility, the DTRMDICL.H header file.

Listing 14.12. The source code for the DTRMDICL.H header file.

```
#if !defined(__dtrmdicl_h)          // Sentry, use file only if
it's not already included.
#define __dtrmdicl_h

/*  Project editor
```

(continues)

Listing 14.12. Continued

```
            Copyright © 1993. All Rights Reserved.

            SUBSYSTEM:    editor.exe Application
            FILE:         dtrmdicl.h
            AUTHOR:


            OVERVIEW
            ========
            Class definition for editorMDIClient (TMDIClient).
*/


#include <owl\owlpch.h>
#pragma hdrstop

#include <owl\opensave.h>

#include "editrapp.rh"               // Definition of all resources.


//{{TMDIClient = editorMDIClient}}
class editorMDIClient : public TMDIClient {
public:
    int                   ChildCount; // Number of child window
                                      // created.

    editorMDIClient ();
    virtual ~editorMDIClient ();

    void OpenFile (const char *fileName = 0);

private:
    void LoadTextFile ();

//{{editorMDIClientVIRTUAL_BEGIN}}
protected:
    virtual void SetupWindow ();
//{{editorMDIClientVIRTUAL_END}}

//{{editorMDIClientRSP_TBL_BEGIN}}
protected:
    void CmFilePrint ();
    void CmFilePrintSetup ();
    void CmFilePrintPreview ();
    void CmPrintEnable (TCommandEnabler &tce);
    void EvDropFiles (TDropInfo);
//{{editorMDIClientRSP_TBL_END}}
DECLARE_RESPONSE_TABLE(editorMDIClient);
};    //{{editorMDIClient}}


#endif                                      // __dtrmdicl_h sentry.
```

The header file in Listing 14.12 contains the declaration of class
editorMDIClient. The class editorMDIClient represents the MDI client area of
the editor. The class uses the member ChildCount to store the number of MDI
child windows. The class declares a constructor, a destructor, and a set of files
to handle various commands, of which most are related to commands of the
File menu.

Summary

This chapter presented basic information regarding the ObjectWindows class
hierarchy, as well as Windows-related information. In this chapter, you
learned about the following topics:

■ The general categories of the OWL class sub-hierarchies.

■ Responding to Windows messages in your own ObjectWindows applications. This process involves declaring descendant ObjectWindows
   classes that contain one or more message-response member functions.
   These functions provide the required response.

■ Defining and sending user-defined messages, then responding to them.

■ Working with sample OWL programs ranging from a minimal OWL
   program to an AppExpert-generated text editor.

Index

We'd Like to Hear from You!

In a continuing effort to produce the highest-quality books possible, Que would like to hear your comments. As radical as this may sound for a publishing company, we **really** want you, the reader and user, to let us know what you like and dislike about this book, and what we can do to improve this book and future books.

In order to provide the most service to you, Prentice Hall Computer Publishing now has a forum on CompuServe (type **GO QUEBOOKS** at any prompt) through which our staff and authors are available for questions and comments. In addition to visiting our forum, feel free to contact me personally on CompuServe at 70714,1516, send your comments, ideas, or corrections to me by fax at (317) 581-4663, or write to me at the address below. Your comments will help us to continue publishing the best books on the market.

Bryan Gambrel,
Product Development Specialist
Que
201 W. 103rd Street
Indianapolis, IN 46290

Disk Offer

The Borland C++ programs in this book are available on disk from the author. The cost of the disk is $6 in the U.S. and Canada, and $10 for overseas orders. Please make your check payable to **Namir Shammas.** When ordering outside the U.S., send a check drawn on a U.S. bank. Sorry, no purchase orders or credit cards.

Name _____

Company (for company address) _____

Address _____

City _____

State or province _____

ZIP or postal code _____

Please specify disk size:

      $5 \frac{1}{4}$ inch _____

      $3 \frac{1}{2}$ inch _____

This offer is made by Namir Shammas, not by Que Corporation.